IRIS LITERARY JOURNAL

VOLUME I, ISSUE 2 - SUMMER 2020

Iris Literary Journal

Volume I, Issue 2 - Summer 2020

Cover Art by Karen Starrett

Iris Literary Journal is published quarterly in print and ebook.

Each journal includes poetry, short fiction, creative nonfiction, drama, and visual art--which includes photography. Some of the work may not be entirely in English.

For more information, visit the website of *Iris Literary Journal*:

www.assurepress.org/iris

An imprint of Assure Press Publishing & Consulting, LLC

www.assurepress.org

Publisher's Note: Assure Press books may be purchased for educational, business, or sales promotional use. For information please visit the website.

ISBN-13: 978-1-7356923-2-6
eISBN-13: 978-1-7356923-3-3

CONTENTS

CREATIVE NONFICTION

VISUAL ART GALLERY

FICTION

DRAMA

Iris Literary Journal

Volume I, Issue 2 - Summer 2020

PURITY

POEMS

Love Bird

-J V Birch

I pick at the tape
careful to tear the paper whole

These are all mine
I must have been good
a doll who can cry
a pony with plaits
books about flower and fairies

The next pile appears like a dream

After I lay them all out
count how much I am loved

She Left Me

-Stephanie Blanch-Byer

calm sassafras
  in
    brown paper bags, a
glare like dry ice.

turn off and turn on

chitterlings
turnip AND mustard greens

dimples.

a laugh from the barrel's bottom of my soul,
twinkle
don't play
Don't Quit
    on my desk,1995
kindness
love wide
    enough
to never throw anyone away
pain alchemized
now, goal after goal after goal met,
                                        CHECK.
forgiveness on a fault line
martyrdom tatted on my soul
and a travel itch not often scratched

hugs to heal a heart hemorrhaging
the beauty shop
entrepreneurship 101
  credit card WTFs
survival mentality with a
thriver's heart . . .
and,
    taste

I Left you

-Stephanie Blanch-Byer

I left
  the darn blueprint tucked
snuggly under your favorite
  Winnie the Pooh pillow
with rhythms synced at 432
no, Hz.
with the blocks to be building
of what best moves would come
from you next
frequencies frequented
528, i love yous
in syrupy abundance
I left plenty of tissue
rubber bands and glue.
Not many to dos, plenty
flashing signs at the
Beginning middle AND end of
                those roads,
you always been hard headed chil'

I left you this mirror
  to help you get it together
sobering , huh?
like I said, I left you this mirror
and, this key.
Now, my dear
live

Pieces of Humanity

-Stephanie Blanch-Byer

The evolution of We from everyone,
to only blood-related family, to friends;
Sorors, to sisters, to my sista girls, and SiStar Goddesses;
the entire black family, ma'at HOTEP! I'm black and I'm proud.
Eventually though, We end up back at
One.

I think, *how can 24 year old me be so dumb?*
Especially sitting next to 14 year old me, who,
by We, meant all of the humanity.
Then, tied up by lies HisStory tells,
We, became smaller and smaller
till We was relegated to the socio-political
assignments divvied to me..
So at 23, We, was black,
and queer, and woman, and poor,
no, middle-class, no poor . . . Well,
let's just say, on that assignment - jury's still out.
By 24 We, was clear.

I wake up.

We, is not a box or a choice.
We,just is.
and, We remembered that We
isn't small.
We is black, and queer,
and smart, and woman,
and man, and *straight*,
and poor, and rich and is
all the royal bits around in and between.
We is what 14 year old me knew 20 plus years ago.

Anew

-Gavin Bourke

In the chapel of apparitions,
intense silence of such balance,
but for the natural creak
of any building,
in the fresh September gusts.

Could hear the heartbeat
echoing in the area,
to the white sculpted angels
and golden crowned goddess.

Swirling, protecting the lamb
of god and cross,
for the penitents and celebrants.
Rhythmical whispers,
layers upon layers.

The brightest light through the glass arch,
broken into constituent colours,
spectrums of variation in the searing quiet.
Background humming of daily anxieties,
over the holy river of purest rain
filtered through rock and humanity.

The gift of peace to the common substratum's,
of the soul's well-springs.
Drenched, reinvented,
renewed in reverence.

The Flamenco Rehearsal

-Jill Bronfman

The first dancer, wearing jeans and a sweatshirt, taps her taps in a diagonal across the stage
She is smiling
But she is serious
The music is illuminating the Palau de la Música Catalana
And her taps are the colors

The second dancer wears a black skirt and stops to sing a few bars, leaning over the musicians and
Brushing her breasts against their chairs
The director, after waving his arms for them to stop, leaps upon the stage, and sings it himself
His vest belies his confidence
His shoes are stiffer leather and keep telling him to slow down

The stage is cleared, the schoolchildren will arrive soon
I am waiting, past the time allowed
Waiting for the lights to go down but they never do
I can't stop tapping my toe and humming a tune I will never remember
Except for the feeling that I have sung and I have danced here with my own body

Transplanting Service

-Lin Marshall Brummels

> "In my Father's house are many mansions: if it were not so, I would have told you. I go to prepare a place for you."
>
> — JOHN 14.2

Hostas flourish on the north
side of my house

Cool temps delay spring shoots'
arrival back there in the shade

Plants poke through the ground
well after the last frost,

like late arrivals for church
avoid shaking hands

One overgrown Hosta needs
to be divided, moved this year.

I locate a new home for this beauty,
push my shovel deep into dark

loam again and again to dig
spacious lodging Set clods aside

Kneel, head bowed to the task,
crumble, massage lumps,

loosen, remove stubborn
dandelion, purslane, fireweed,

murmur a prayer for transplants
One plant becomes many,

filling the multitude
of carefully arranged spaces

Settle in place, cover with dirt
This backyard mansion

waits for them, mourning dove
choir fills the air with song,

compost donation concludes
this Sunday ritual.

Through My Window, Kuwait City, 1995

-Anna Citrino

Filled with heat, the world was empty of plants,
trees or weeds. Three years before there'd been
a war. Landmines and shells still waited atop roofs,

beside downtown towers, and beneath the Gulf,
though we couldn't see them.
Instead, we saw the sun's light cascading

down the lace of the Imam Hussein mosque's
intricately decorated white stone towers,
shining walls and embroidered angles.

Five times a day, prayers streamed
from the mosque's green dome across the desert,
longing pressed into the city's myriad walls.

What stories the Imam told beneath the dome
to the thousands gathered there, to shape the minds
and hearts of those who listened, I didn't know,

but I felt the rhythm of the prayers—
the building's beauty teaching me
how light takes form and shapes us.

The Secret

after "La Confidence," Elizabeth Jane Gardner Bougereau

-Jane Costain

She pulls her friend close to whisper in her ear.
In her hand, a paper with pressed flowers.
A note from someone? A love note?

So serious, their faces, as they share this secret,
one kept all these years. Two girls,
their lives before them. Plenty of time

to learn of love's complications.
For now, just a moment in this summer day---
as innocent as their bare feet.

The Gift

-Jane Costain

The summer he was four
Benjamin lost his turtle
and his goldfish in the same
week. Unwilling to give up,

he decided on a crab for his
new pet. Barely able to reach
the bell, he stood at my door
with chubby confidence

and a request---a seashell
for the crab. I gave him one,
perfect, pink, delicate, that
I had brought many years ago

from a beach in France. That
afternoon he came again,
this time with a small pink,
plastic heart, slightly cracked,

he had found that morning
underneath a chair at the local
swimming pool. He knew
how pleased I would be with it.

A Man and a Dog

-Jane Costain

He stopped to pet a dog, on his way
to somewhere, the man, that is. The dog
knew he was already there and that he
was exactly where he wanted to be---

here, and had long ago stopped trying
to get elsewhere---run away, as he
had done in his youth only to be hauled
back to this place where he was today

when the man stopped. The dog was
happy here. Sometimes someone would
pause but mostly people hurried by,
talking on their little phones to someone

someplace else. The man, a tall man,
was used to bending, but only slightly
to avoid being hit by certain doorjambs
or low-flying birds. He was not used

to stopping, always having to be some-
where he was not, wherever that might be.
The dog caused the man to almost double
over to scratch that place behind the ears

that dogs like. This was new for the man,
this position of little importance but
important to a dog who liked to be petted.
As the man's ear drew closer to the dog,

he heard a strange, high-pitched sound---
someone was speaking to him. Not the dog.
That would be absurd, but someone was
asking him in a barely audible voice,

"Where are you going?" And then he knew
what the dog already knew---he had never
been going anywhere really and that was
how it had always been and always would be.

Game with No Game

-RC deWinter

i've game for love
but i've got no game
in the realm of romance

no tricks
no spectacular legerdemain
in my dealings with the heart

i lay myself on the line
and get run over every time
passion's roadkill
on that lonely midnight highway

what you see is what you get
but there are no takers
somehow i missed out
on the wisdom of deceit
of using cruelty and the tease
as the sure means to an end

so call me naïve
call me victim
but never call me liar or cheat

and if that's what i take with me
alone
to bed at night
well
surely there are worse ways to live

Sin of Innocence

-RC deWinter

i remember my first cup of coffee not allowed at home
gloria's mother poured us each a thimbleful in a grownup cup filled
to the brim with milk giggling feeling sophisticated though at six
we didn't know that word we drank it but that night in bed with
my conscience i couldn't sleep for worrying about dying going to hell
and the robin's nest falling from a wormy apple tree and how when i
tried to put those naked hatchlings back i killed them with my clumsy
good intentions another stain on a soul steeped in the body and the
blood
anything that wasn't pure and good was a checkmark for the devil
and the
crush i had on the boy next door when i was five and he was ten
and more guilt for wanting to kiss him

Flambeaux

-RC deWinter

the sky   an
unbroken egg of
robin's blue
  my heart a
deeper shade   beats in rhythm
with coming midnight

  somewhere a
cello plays counter
point   bowed by
a strong man's
hand   caressing every note
with unquestioning

devotion
  the fidelity
of fearless
surrender
  distance obviates any
conjunction   left to

imagine
what fires we could start
  i let go
of the day
  seeking salvation in a
tactical retreat
lying down
  my fingers matchsticks
lighting those
fires along
the periphery of an

unknown landscape the

cello sings
in the forest of
my bones your
breath the wind
  sending bright sparks into the
velvet of the night

The Jook and the Blues

-donnarkevic

Dad told me, "Will, never, never . . ."
and this woman sits, hand on my thigh,
presses her red lips against my ear,
asks me why she has no drink,
and I think, 'Dad told me, Will, never . . .'
and she smells like hyacinth,
her flowery dress blooming,
her breasts, and Dad told me
about the jook and the ladies,
but he had no words
for the fragrance and the silky
sleeve brushing against my arm,
how a mere shoulder movement
draws attention back to her breasts,
and another man lights
her cigarette, the smoke blown
in my direction, the chair next to me
empty again as a church pew,
and the music stops, and the noise
of boys shooting craps,
Dad told me, "Will, never, never . . ."
and the guitar player asks
why I'm so blue, like I just fell
off the sheet music
played at a funeral, how he turns
the chair around, sits, says don't
friend that gal and admires my shoes,
says no one should look down
at brown leather two-tones
and look up to see such a sad ass,
and I think, 'Dad told me, Will, never. . .'
so, I don't know if the dude insulted me

or just called a spade a spade,
anyway, he asks me my age,
advises me to leave
before I get into trouble
with a woman or her man
or a crap game gone bad,
and I ask him who he thinks he is,
and he says he's a dad who sings
the blues over a child he never knew
and how he hopes to live long enough
to see the end of the year, and how
he hopes the same for me, too.

The Broach

-donnarkevic

Fussy about details, my daughter
notices it, a rhinestone broach
my Ciocia Mary wore on her
blazer lapel. *My first gift*
from Uncle Eddie, she explains,
Christmas Eve, 1950, the date,
an imaginary number
to an eight-year-old,
an eternity to Mary,
those years since
his death.

Her hand crossed her heart
to touch the piece, a bauble
of inflorescent glass, love
in eternal bloom, present
as the day he offered
to pin it to her blouse,
his hands trembling
until her hand crossed
her heart and steadied
his tremor.

Gifts left for us,
Ciocia Mary says to me,
also widowed.

As my restless daughter
reaches for me, signaling
the end of conversation,
her fingers, porcelain petals,
close around my hand,
her tug causing me to look
into her mother's eyes,
precious stones, reflections
of the keepsake of my own,
love, imperishable.

Empty Nest

-donnarkevic

Fallen from an elm, she rescues it,
whirling in an eddy at creek's edge.
No hatchlings remain.

In the cup of her wing-hands,
my daughter presents the find
like an offering to the god of flight.

With her fingers, thin as twigs
she traces the intricate weave
as I explain the creation of found art.

After inspection, she saddens,
wanting to return it to a place
where it will abide forever.

To provide shelter and protection
for jays or wrens, she chooses
a thorny thicket of raspberries.

When my daughter pricks a thumb,
she rejects consolation, and I marvel
with regret at her tearless eyes.

STRANGER

-Ken Farrell

Another 3am I spend channel surfing
and as the inky hour turns
I know I should be sleeping.
My four-year-old son will grab me by the toe
and drag me from bed at 6am
regardless of my jaunts
in Sam Hell's Frog Town,
despite my mop jousts as *The Toxic Avenger*,
so I rise deliriously tired
and shuffle to the kitchen
to make pancakes, and in a voice gruffly
not his own, my boy challenges me
to a light-saber duel, repeating
you're not my father while I struggle
to place the dance of the three snakes
to discover who moved the sink
to remember flour doesn't belong
in the fridge, milk doesn't belong
in the cupboard. *You're not my father*
the accusation flies;
in a borrowed voice I reply
I am your father. Come to the dark side
and he smiles, but I suspect I am suspect,
a stranger in this static-free world,
and as the griddle heats and his mom
descends the stairs, I apprehend I am
a creature crossed over from the dark side—
a land illumined by cathode rays alone:
a land where sunrise
is something to be suspicious of.

Mother Gothel

-Olga Gonzalez Latapi

flowers would not doubt
&
give us answers even as
lily lights
dance & take our
own reflection
where first stars
still part the
skies

John's Smile

-Cleo Griffith

When you smile,
I cannot stop smiling.

I could find a frown deep inside –
there's always one that lurks
between the heart and the backbone,
but the smile is so contagious,
even to yourself, that you chuckle.
I hug you and you make a humming sound.

Away from you, sorrow can bring a tear.
I never fear but let it fall,
feel its coolness.
It cannot chill
the appreciation for your lack of self-pity,
your lightness, brightness and laughter.

You smile,
everyone smiles.

Burying Adam

-Patrick Cabello Hansel

Across the vast, unnamed plains,
two sons sing by the heaving earth:
the one who had given her lineage,
the one who had walked out
calling on the ground to cease
its howling for blood. Eve must
call to them now. Their meat
and grain, the memory
of their walk, the tools
they have invented against death.

The keening, the sprinkling
with dust, the fires
and flowers of fools,
all these come later.
There is still time
to marvel at the stillness
of Adam's lip, the soft fold
near his nose, his open eye,
God's promise come due at last.

She kneels on the ground.
She becomes the dusk,
a broken window into heaven.
Slowly,
with her hands, with the name
he had given her,
she begins to wash the skin
of this earth, this husband,
this wound without a voice.

Ruth at Naomi's Bedside

-Patrick Cabello Hansel

These feet that walked our grief
from land to land, now lie
cracked and shrunken on the mat.
Mother, sister, friend. Your eyes
have stopped longing for another
world, and have begun to
inhabit it: trees whose leaves
never fall, grain as abundant
as the dust we trod, songs
sung in each creature's tongue.

( )

I take your hand,
wrinkled, but soft.
Breath enters your nose,
then something like a word,
given but not spoken
escapes your lips. It passes
between us like a star.
Mother, sister, friend.
Your heart rises and falls
as the tide; the scent of
your skin billows the sky.
Do not leave me
or forsake me. Yes,
I have my husband
and my child. But
only you have me.

Emergency

-Patrick Cabello Hansel

The blue paper gown was too large
for the little one's body, and so
it billowed into the bright air of the ER
like a welcoming sea. The nurses
had pierced the first vein they found,
swiftly and with little pain, and
the fluid in the hanging bag spilled,
drop by drop, into her whispering blood.
She sat on her mother's lap, unaware
of the great flood still waiting to flow
from the silent face above her, a face
with no desire but to have this child,
and to hold her, this morning, forever.

The little one's eyes had shuddered
but an hour before, like a stylus
mapping tremors along the fault line
of this beloved rock, floating on
on top of a restless, boiling lake,
bequeathed to us by our sun.
Her body had tightened to an iron rod
banging on the air and sounds like strange
birds dying came from her mouth and
wakened her father. He shouted for his
wife and older daughter to rise, to keep
weeping, yes, but move fast, get your
clothes on, as the overheated blood
of this child, this unknowable blessing
continued to rumble her brain, a gift
from her creator, who had anticipated
such terror even before flesh was
created, and made convulsions,

the shaking of the body by the swirling
of the brain, into a kind of noble
but frightening baptism: fire to put
out fire, a deluge of sparks to calm
the unknowable, dark depths.

The doctor counseled a spinal tap,
to rule out blood in the brain,
to give assurance to himself and
the little one's parents by piercing
the long river that carries each call
and response to every cell in every
part of the body. The parents
nodded their nervous "yes",
and held each other like worn
life vests. Mother stayed with
the blue billowed girl, as her

ten-year old sister—who had
temporarily forgotten the terror
that had thrown her out of sleep—
got incredibly bored and was
looking for something, anything to
amuse herself with. Old *Highlights*
for Children on the side table,
toys for children a bit older than her
beloved sister, but ones that no self
respecting tweener would touch;
she wrestled with her hands and feet,
until her father sat on the carpet
next to her, and started flipping
the letters on the spin-a-letter
rack, making up crazy phrases:
aardvark sinuses, and pumpkin
butts and several that ended in poop
and as they laughed and tried

to outdo each other with weird,

all the saints of Saint Christopher's
Hospital for Children on East
Allegheny Street in Philadelphia,
the nurses in their smocks colored
with cartoon characters, the orderlies
emptying trash cans and wheeling
children to X-Ray and therapy,
the line cooks in the cafeteria
deep in the bowels of the building
preparing post-surgery treats,
and even the flying giraffes

and the monkeys in tutus and
baseball caps painted on the walls,
lifted up the little one onto
their shoulders, and began
to carry her across the river.

Torchbearers

-Jeanne Julian

There was one man, but he was not among us.
Hired to drive the truck, repair whatever broke
or stuck, he lived in the farmhouse down the road
with his wife and family. The rest of us were female,

at that rustic camp in Ohio's southern hills.
We bunked in screened cabins, treehouses, tents.
Beside our metal cots, fruit crates served as shelves.
Electricity was scarce. By flash- and lantern-light

we'd walk to the toilets, scuffing flip-flops noisily
to ward off raccoons, skunks, along the gravel path
posted with spigots. From these we'd fill canteens
with spring water, metallic-tasting, clean and cold.

Meals, plain fare prepared by local women,
were served family style. We took turns clearing plates.
The rare offer of an orange Fanta from the office cooler
seemed like a sip of civilization, those humid days.

We were far removed from TV, fast food, gyms,
and shopping, we girls, we women, dwelling together
beside the small brown lake, sheltered by hemlocks.
Here is what we taught and learned and made:

how to gather tinder, kindling, fuel. How to build
a fire—our aim a one-match blaze.
How to cook a supper wrapped in foil,
embedded in hot coals and ash.

How to row a boat, rescue someone drowning.
How to climb a cliff face and belay.
How to tell poison ivy from Virginia creeper,
find tasty leaves of teaberry on the forest floor.

How to make a tabletop by lashing
twine and sticks, hew logs into benches.
How to craft a wooden-covered book.
How to raise a flag, lower and fold it.

How to sing in harmony a capella, and singing,
how to hike just one more mile in the heat.
How to find the Pleiades, Cassiopeia,
help a city child lose her dread of darkness.

How to craft torches from long branches
topped with kerosene-soaked rags and, as night fell
in the woods, hold them high as young girls
processed, wide-eyed, through an arcade of glow.

Don't get me wrong: I know many who face
challenges more severe, ace more salient skills.
But sometimes when I think "I can't," I recall
lessons from those rugged summer sojourns, and how

the huge boulder that leaned, a menacing Gibraltar,
over the dusty entrance road was—so legend had it—
propped up, magically, by a host of twigs gathered
and placed upright there by girlish hands, their hands alone.

Compensation

-Jeanne Julian

After grad school,
she clerked at a shop
stocked with tchotchkes,
books, and greeting cards.
She did not mind her work
of tidying: not hard to keep
With Deepest Sympathy
out of the slots assigned
to *Happy Birthday*
and to ensure *Get Well*
contained no *Congratulations.*
Her reward, a half-sleep at the register.

Along the back wall lurked
ranks of men's magazines extolling
vehicles and games—decoys,
among *Playboy, Juggs,* and *Swank*
purveying slick scenes
of jumbo-breasted women
lolling upon fur, sucking lollipops,
a shameless sameness she ignored
(after checkout, easily tucked
by lustful sirs inside
folded *Barron's* investment news
or the *Daily Racing Form*).

In corners, stuck on wire racks,
the dated Wharton, Woolf, and Angelou—
even lordly Stephen King—
faded and dimmed beneath dust.
She was allowed to choose,

acquire, any paperback
for free, provided she first
stripped off and saved
the covers for inventory.
And so mutilated
books lined her own shelves,
defaced, but spine intact.

The Oldest Poet

In memory of Tom Blow

-Jeanne Julian

In our coffeehouse he found a friendly
forum for his humor, rhyme, and meter,
a gray, hunched, suspendered, humble reader
unfazed by slam, slang, and modernity.
At 96, he began his mornings
thinking "What shall I write about today?"—
long memory providing much to say
and smile about, until, without warning,
he could no longer share his words or life
with other poets, those who understood.
It's all I knew of him: those Tuesday nights.
To me, he's like a cottage in dark woods,
quaint, seen from afar, where a window light
tells passing strangers to believe in Good.

Pastels

-Hari Bhajan Khalsa

Bring me a slow walk
in the morning,

dandelions, red wine
in a clear glass, drop

of indigo on a blank canvas,
jasmine in the night—

the things that give
a shiver—oranges fallen

from a tree, a woman's face
wrapped in a scarf, soothing

hands on the ache
in your heart. In a dream,

my mother, face close-up
like the Buddha in scarlet

lipstick. No need to apologize
for the sentiment, lament

the way you're built.
Take long strides. Float

in your sea, chest bared,
cracked wide open.

Something Dying Something Being Born

-Hari Bhajan Khalsa

Ache down the left
side of my head,

the jaw takes
the brunt. What's going

on? They say the body
has answers,

mine only questions—
in my thighs,

mouth in a downward
trajectory, fingers

furiously translating.
I couldn't tell you what.

The swarm of,
shudder of, little tensions

like, you know, how sparks
go off, jump from pole

to pole, split atoms,
joints flex and extend,

rush back to stasis, flowers
in full bloom folding

in at dusk.
It seems best to run

to conversations of why,
forget the *how's*

it going to be—look
out the window—the pines,

black-capped chickadee,
the scuffling clouds.

What Birds Know

-Hari Bhajan Khalsa

When you wake and begin
to curse yourself for what

you did or didn't do
the day before in the realm

of what you consider
to be right, remember who

you're talking to and tilt
towards kindness. Birds

do this instinctively, mother
birds, even when it's raining,

the nest soggy, laden
and the chicks huddle,

mouths wide, baby bird
wide, chirping to be fed

and fed again, in the most
urgent way possible

and she scans, waits for a break
in the clouds to set off,

to hunt. It stands to reason
they feel—the aging

falcon mourns loss
of its keenness, a dove

knows sorrow, mockingbird
the thrill of its song.

Love Bird

-Paul Kurzeja

Remember when I gave you my canary at the restaurant?
I took it from my heart shaped cage
and held it out to you in my open hand.
Vulnerable and new.
You gave a slanted smile and looked away,
then settled your darting eyes on your drink.
You swirled the glass in your hand,
ice rattled the rim.
Then you asked a passing waiter for a refill.

The little, yellow bird fluttered about the table
not knowing where to go.
It paused atop the votive,
balanced above the flame.
I was afraid the fire would leap up and consume it,
but it only gave a forlorn flicker.

The bird darted across the restaurant,
frightened and confused.
It landed on the hostess stand and looked at me,
eyes lost and sad,
then flew out the open door.

As I walked you home,
I hoped the bird might appear.
When it did not, I thought it might return to its cage in the night.
But when I looked, my cage was empty.

What They Want To Hear

-ky li

WHAT THEY WANT TO HEAR

Mother was born where the mountains dip their toes
into the Kentucky River, where grass that is emerald
has been christened blue, vowels sound in twos & locals
preach an alloy of the Golden Rule — *say unto others*
as you would have them say unto you. I first learned this
when they smothered the funeral parlor in roses for Granny.
A spray of Forever Young tried to squeeze her wilted body
from the open casket; her face resembled a pale reduction
of chicken stock. One mourner said, *Don't she look nice?*
to which my six-year-old mouth said, *No, she looks dead!*
Mother smiled through teeth kept white with salt, bent down
to my level & whispered, *always tell folk what they want to hear.*
I found my way through nyloned legs & polyester pants
to a back room & the almost-honest smell of formaldehyde.

Into Red Metal

for William Carlos Williams

-ky li

His words were lengthened by clouds
that moved in & out of blue & being.

They bled into veins of truth like ore
in a granite face, washed into gullies
over singing stones of brooks, filtered
into red metal & polished into tomes
to be read & reread, cited & recited by
mouths uninitiated in cloud & blue, by
ears unaccustomed to stone melodies
& eyes that see being as something to
touch. There is no interpreter, no code
to be broken, only words lengthened &
measured by an hourglass whose sand
once formed the face of a granite peak.

Sydney (Reflections)

-Laura Lucas

in a room with mirrors
for walls we noticed
our subtle
womanhood
scolded the images
of bodies that break
and burn
in the white light of a world
that never learned
the meaning of beauty
my youth huddled
in the corner
large and nostalgic
staring brutishly at our
sacred monuments
our proof of arrival
in this room with mirrors
for walls
you laughed
at how many people there are
in the world and i counted
the lines on my thighs
wishing away that white
light

Moon Dream

-Laura Lucas

in a dream i watched the moon rise
she filled the dark sky
with audible light
musical moon beams
i thought she might swallow me
whole
all i could do was
stare
surrender
keep drinking
her light
until my heart sang
too

LATE JULY

-Carol Louise Munn

Early morning is almost cool,
dark skies turn gray
as an afternoon in winter
before a line of pink
spreads through the trees.

I am alone in a world
transforming every day.

Before eating, my cat waits
for my hand to scratch his ears,
for me to say his name.

I call my great-aunt,
hear her weep as life
clings to her like the pink
bathrobe she was reduced
to wearing to breakfast.

She asks me to lend her
patience to wait until she sees sun
from the other side of heaven.

Nelle, I speak
her earthly name
Nelle.

A Cinema with a Courtyard

-Robert Nisbet

It's just a child's imagination, they all said,
when she came back from visiting Wales,
crossing from Ireland to Fishguard and the Gwaun,
in Britain's slowly-stirring post-war years.
She'd seen, she told them, miles and miles inland,
a cinema with a courtyard, a wonderful place,
great furniture stores around the square,
places to walk, and not just the movies (Reagan
in the B feature) but the graciousness.
She'd been told the cinema had operas,
Robeson had been, singers like that. O city life.

You were a kid, Ellie, you were only eight, they said.
It was some local flea-pit you've exaggerated.
But Ellie, retired, her relatives gone, searched records.
Cardiff? Queen Street? Not really. Swansea's Odeon?
Hardly. Llanelli? Carmarthen even?

But she found it, fifteen miles inland from Fishguard:
The County Theatre in Haverfordwest,
there, in photos, looking much as she remembered it.
The Cavendish Showroom beside a wide arcade.
The mass, the sturdiness of the place, the imposing worth.
The river to the right, and local operetta certainly,
and yes, Isobel Baillie sang with Robeson there,
on May the first in 1938.

It stood for half a century, pulled down in time
for council offices. There was little fuss
because its grandeur was unfashionable,
nineteen-thirties-brick-built, in a Georgian town.
But for an Irish farm girl, growing up, a drudge,
it was her amulet of grace, youth's glorious icon.

Aubade

-Shana Ross

We wake in darkness, stuffed into the room.

The child craves immersion in the unfamiliar. The father-husband wants to run. I decide the literal interpretation, do not slice myself with loneliness. Also he wants to show us the mountains. I clutch tender. The Leonids are expected, peaking just before dawn. I coax the child. Quick, quick, we will all go together.

Full moon. Total cloud cover. Light enough to obscure the stars, light itself mostly hidden. We go anyway. Into the foothills, dark covers the outlines of the rising earth. Incline of road, some shoulder, passing trucks. We follow the GPS, which is one way to know where you are or where you are not. We arrive.

We walk. Into the trail, into the dark, phone light spilling. To turn them off, we all need to agree, to surrender in entirely equal measure. In the same moment. We adjust slowly. Finally we are floating in the light of glowing cloud, the halo where we infer the moon, the dawn we think is coming. Husband and I lean into each other – seeking, offering, our vectors balance. Our deep breaths taste like nothing. I was sure that pine could be swallowed like creosote or crisping oak leaves. The sky seems unchanged, but now the rocks remember themselves. This is dawn. Contrast rising and warming like arousal, slowly, predictably and unique to this day.

Pity for the bored child, the cold child, the boy who binds his whining tight to his chest but want for breakfast leaks out. Revelation comes in color, a language we struggle to dream in. The turquoise of this elevation is new to me. Night falls away, slips down the mountains and we head for the early bird breakfast buffet with an omelet station. We say yes to both donuts and froot loops and this is already the best day ever and we are the best parents and what about orange juice? My husband and I drink terrible coffee and smile at each other across the high top. No, *this*, this is finally dawn.

Starstruck

-Shana Ross

I paid online then went into the tank
wondering what I might learn from resting
all senses, but I could not stop feeling

the water around me. *Stubborn body,*
said the woman, adjusting things in the machine
I resist silence but don't say much either

learning to immerse in discomfort is practice
for the world to come – by which I mean time
gnawing at your identity, I mean civilization

determined to crack into ever sharper teeth,
I mean death, coming, eventually, as it does.
I could not manage to fool myself into leaving

the world behind even for a forty minute session
discounted in the unpopular hours. Now it is
nearly spring again, or maybe we have already crossed

that boundary. I sleep shallow in colorless dreams.
On rising, a voice: *well aren't you starstruck?*
But it's dawn. A friend tells me we don't

really hear voices in our heads, we remember them
as if they had sounded. It isn't dawn. The birds
have been singing since just after four, by now

the blue of the sky has resolved itself.

When God Prays

-Shana Ross

God wraps their tefillin a little too tight
worries that their love is seen as something
to be suffered, both for what it is and will be

but is not yet, in this world. God tries to put aside
all thoughts other than intention when
God prays. Sometimes the shuffle, back and forth,

the showing up, is all God can manage,
and God wonders if this is enough.
God does not enter the ruins to pray

we have already established, there are demons
and debris might fall, not to mention
all the assumptions others might make

if they see God sneaking around the abandoned
places. Better stick to the road, cut things short.
God tries to carry holiness into the day ahead

after having to look up the word phylacteries
because God keeps forgetting how to say things
in English that have no business being translated

when the good words could be imported whole
and now there is not enough time for coffee,
not enough time to savor the coffee, the bitter and the hot

sip after sip, hands warming, staring into the distance
in preparation for whatever comes, no there's only enough
time to drink quickly, for caffeine and not kavannah -

but that's the way it is, some days. God still feels wrapped
a little too tight, tension held, but no way to let go
like the rabbi who went rock climbing and discovered

when you reach the top, you only have two choices:
let go on purpose, or wait until you give out and fall.
Either way, the rope is ready for you, and your ride

is waiting to lower you steadily to the ground.
God forgets to make time for hobbies, some days.
I, most days, wrestle until it is time to rest.

Still Life with Lemons, Oranges and a Rose

Francisco de Zurbaran, 1633 (Norton Simon Museum)
-Mary Kay Rummel

Three ripe lemons reflected
in a plate of polished pewter —
breast shaped ovals in morning light,
shadows defined
by slanted autumn sun on stones.

Ancient motifs — the trinity, homages to the virgin —
oranges with blossoms, water in pewter for purity,
the thornless rose, shades of white and tissue pink,
immaculate conception to renaissance viewers.

It's the intensity of color that draws me,
that curls my fists and fingers,
lemony oil, pocked yet smooth skin.
My mouth tightening at the taste.

Round bellied oranges wear deeper shadows,
as do sinners who bite into fruit.

The background, obsidian
color beyond all colors, living pigment
created at the back of the brain,
bright as the history of shadows.
Each color a kaleidoscope
muted with gothic dark.

She Loved Him the Way He Used to Be

-Joel Savishinsky

She loved him the way he used to be,
his current incarnation a postcard
reminder to check out the past,
keep it in mind for future reference.

Her memories of him were mostly dark matter,
scraped from the unlit side of his life,
the cratered schemes he mislabeled dreams.

It only seemed to have been a choice later on.
At the time she'd made her move, the tides and
the Jetstream were crushing people inside
their lives, leaving them full of thoughts but
bereft of ways and means with which to say them.

Sitting alone on late afternoons now,
she found herself staring, dismembered,
disarmingly calm, ready for the next crazy.

ADOPTION: FOUR, EIGHT, TWELVE

-Joel Savishinsky

Math is not her best
subject, but she is
very good at counting
all her grandparents
and cousins.

Language is a stronger
suit. She knew, at four, all
the names she had borne
since birth, and liked to
say the ones her first parents
carried away.

When the couple who took
her in and out of
harm's way split themselves
apart, separating homes and
branches, in that single

small season her thin
eight-year-old tree of
a body knew more
new growth than most
fatted kings can claim
from history's vineyards.

She has dimensionality.
Despite the soil, she is
fierce at forcing roots.
At twelve, she asked
all the elders she could
to watch her play soccer.
With a rare gift of grace,
eight complied, housed for
an autumn afternoon

on two rows of
steel bleachers, talking
about her at half-time
as if life's inequities --
their quarterly reports and
and moonlighting paystubs --
were someone else's fiction.

Her team lost, but
the photos of her unranked kin
showed the score was not about
the game she had been in.

If This Ride Never Ends: Seattle Transit Bus Route #36

-Joel Savishinsky

What is it to you, he thought,
glancing at the person across
the aisle of the bus, if I do not
bring dinner home or eat it,
if the monsoons erode the sides
of the bare hills and wash the exiles'
table-top tents into the river,
or whether I can or cannot see
the blasted city and the broken,
blood-stained bones of its buildings?

If this ride never ends, I would be
content to escape the fire and
its responsibilities, the taint of
the offerings, and all the odors of regret.

One swipe of my card in the toll box
will take me to forever, sated, seated
in this place that does not stay in place.

Everything lost and lingering

After Malcolm Tariq

-d. n. simmers

In shadows—

Night
is a woven shade.

Darkness is a weave
of black fiber.

Crossing out night, into the light of day.

As if
two sisters change places.

Stitch
in and stitch out.

Light into darkness.

Mind
can be
in the shadows.

Or listening for
first light to
enter and set it free.

Beginnings and endings—

The circle of a
snake

eating itself

trying to escape
and be set free.

Patternmaker

-William R. Stoddart

I see him tiling in the infinite
layers of thin glass. He stands
in the unfinished powder room,

an oasis in a turn of the century cellar:
dirt floor, tree columns, coal cellar
abandoned for the new gas furnace.

I am five years old and afraid of the
coal cellar. Spider webs, coal dust,
I stay close to my grandfather. He's wearing

an A-shirt and suspenders hanging
down along gray trousers. He uses
a straight razor on his chalky face,

mixing the brush in a soap cup.
The barbershop smell steams the mirror.
He is silent as I watch the odd faces

he makes. Holding the straight razor to his
wrinkled throat he sees me out of the
corner of his muddy blue eyes, he smiles

returning to his work. I've never seen
him use the new electric razor
on the shelf above the sink. I think
he uses it when I'm not around. He prefers
to show me the old ways, that's the patternmaker
in him, his foundry apprenticeship

before the war to end all wars. His hand

works the straight razor slowly, then fast
on the throat finishing, cleansing

the dark reflection. He rinses the soap brush
and straight razor, spacing them neatly
along the shelf above the sink. He takes

my hand and shows me the empty coal cellar,
not wanting me to fear it he shovels darkness,
casting fear into the wax pattern of a tender heart.

The Peace of Angels

-William R. Stoddart

Celebrate midwinter's long-traveled light
dear little ones, on this longest of nights.
For all that is immured in purgatorial winter,

for that which we see in our time, all rise
to the darkness above, returning you this place,
this peace. May these celestial pictures

light your way through dark valleys
until you reach transcendent dawn. And when
you look into the vastness of dreams-deferred,

spent years from now, like the slow burn of rust
on the polished surface of a dream,
may it not slow your steps. For now,

breathe in the cold dark of midwinter's night:
sleep the peace of angels my pride,
sleep the peace of angels.

Hide and Seek

-William R. Stoddart

We lean closed eyes into bark-treaded forearms.
Our home base maple tree sways in hot July wind.

Old company houses stand between green lawns
like the sonnet sequence of Arlington stones.

We play between those sepulchral walls
whitewashed safe as duck and cover desks.

Our dog dies hard — tire-treaded in the gutter.
The girls giggle and point — I cry.

The neighbor covers the carcass with burlap.
I recall pictures of tomatoes on the box we buried

in the cool earth and afterward, the languid climb
up the maple to watch the hissing curtain of water

roiling toward me perched high in the tree,
holding the crow's nest trunk, the smell

of wet earth rising, slowly evaporating
like river water from newly minted baptized.

The sun came out and I looked for a rainbow,
but there was just the humid slowness of summer,

and I welcomed the slowness of it,
wishing to Jesus it would never end.

What Does the Future Think?

-Tim Suermondt

> Predictions are hard to make, especially
> if they're about the future.
>
> — *YOGI BERRA*

But we try nonetheless.
Sunlight tells me it will be wonderful—
the storm with high winds and rain
tells me the road may be quite rocky.
I'm on the lookout for both, my window
sturdy and strong and comforting
and in-between I take some books
from the shelves, the lucky ones who
will again be read as the weather keeps
deciding—let the adventures begin.

Summer with Some Pain around

-Tim Suermondt

The man plays a saxophone, badly,
but he gives it his all.

He plays the sax the way I played
the clarinet when I was a boy, certain

that somehow, someway I would rule
the instrument and the world.

After his short performance, the man slings
the sax over his shoulder and meanders down

a deserted alley, on his way to another
corner gig, buoyed yet again

by the knowledge that there's always playing
to do, endless streets to get everything right.

Tuesday

-Tim Suermondt

My wife writes down my doctor's
appointment in the desk calendar—
a lot of care on display in this act.

The machine washer hums beautifully,
seems to revel in the last cycle,
colors galore ready to preen.

The classical music CD has stopped
on cue, the sudden silence giving way
to the fall of rain, one window open.

I'm writing—god knows what—
but I'm writing, surprising myself
as well as you without a hint of sadness.

Under the Volcano

-O. Alan Weltzien

We land at Legazpi Airport, southeast Luzon,
and Mt. Mayon's upper triangle shines
above swirling clouds in dawn light.
Over three days and nights its sightlines
burn my retinas when the clouds pause
and separate from its mass in their westward

journey. According to legend clouds gather
at the crater when the doomed lovers,
Magayon, beautiful maiden, and Pangaronon
kiss. They're buried where Mayon rose.
Its calm marks their embraces; when it
sputters, about to blow, the jealous suitor,

Pagtuga, is challenging Pangaronon. Love
or male jealousy, oldest trope. The most
symmetric volcano on earth after Japan's
Fuji-san, Mayon tapers over 8000'
above city and province. I study
its eastern profile, cloudless after dawn,

from an island and gasp, trace gullies
and ridges, imagine the climb. Desire
wells but so does lava and steam
which keep climbers at bay the past
few years. Most active volcano, it
often flares and vents, rarely asleep

for long. Under it I quake, breathe
steadily, place steps, follow my guide
up a new track to its hot spout:
my fevered dream and its broad,
triangle mass loom long
after airport departure.

Dirty Word

-Sharon Whitehill

We wanted a chance for every human being to be strong and live a life of happiness.

— EMIL SEIDEL, MILWAUKEE MAYOR 1910-12.

a fifty-year Socialist rule
in Milwaukee where I grew up
citywide drinking fountains,
heating and toilets in factories
contagious diseases reduced
green miles of parkland with a lagoon
where my father took me as child
to feed the ducks

at dinner one night in my teens
I praised socialism as an ideal

my father's fist hit the table
making the silverware jump
his passion traceable
to the tale of himself at fifteen
having listened impressed
to a street-corner socialist's logic
and repeated it all to *his* father
who sandblasted clean
of seditious ideas, polished him up
to a grateful patina
for an enlightenment
that kept its gloss through the years

that same treatment imposed on me
failed to silver my mind
to a mirror reflecting his own
instead melted me down
left my intellect weak as a paperclip
too often bent back and forth

as the fear of being denounced
laundered Milwaukee
of left-wing political views
so the dirtiest word in my childhood home
scrubbed away by my father
built up in me again
like dust in the corners
my father could no longer reach

CREATIVE NONFICTION

SOUTHPAW BELLY DANCER

BELLABIANCA LYNN

SUEDE WITH A HINT OF CARPET LIFTS INTO MY NOSE FROM HANDS AND knees. My yoga mat and I are an island in my living room. These simple, though not easy, yoga movements of pelvic tilts are a prerequisite to my belly dance warm-up. In tilting my head up, one yoga instructor comes to mind: “Even out the pressure across your hands.” From a neutral spine, I hear another: “No white fingernails but no sharp pain in the wrist, either.” Oy with the seesaw teaching already!

Burning muscles stretch across shoulders, forearms, and hands. But I press into patience. The fluidity needed in my fingers will wake up. Then I can find my dancing body.

As a forty-eight-hour-old baby, I suffered a stroke on my brain’s left side, resulting in cerebral palsy, a sort of muscle paralysis on my right side. As the way opposites work, my right brain took the rest of me under its wings and acted as a surrogate as the left brain healed itself. From day two, I’ve been quite the left-handed, right-brain adapter: learning to text one-handed during flip phone days, shaving dominant limbs, and five-finger-keyboard typing (but roughly 80 words a minute!).

What exactly is the prescription that loosens my right fingers? Keeping my thumb open across the suede. In the secret hour of dawn, I know that I’m not the only one whose joints don’t open or close first thing in the morning. But I may be one of the few whose joints have found it hard to open from the beginning.

My life's beginning does not change. But what can is where the beginning wanders off to and how it moves through time. Free-writing around my hand inadequacies allows me to access one of my younger moments of struggle with my right side: I sit outside at recess with my arm shelled, covered by my left, in anticipation of the bell ringing. Weight across it quiets the jerking motion that resembled kickback from a gun. Writing about right-sided struggles is where being one kind of southpaw becomes a fighting southpaw through voice.

I approached a belly dance class out of curiosity, curious about its benefits, and curious about the choreography. Could I even do it? I whispered to myself. But upon my first lesson, I discovered that I was a southpaw by way of leading with the right side of my body, my left learning under its guidance. My own internal surrogate family still there for me after twenty-two years.

> "Belly dancer is an archetype that cuts deep. To embrace that archetype, it's like a key [...] all this forgotten stuff about living life comes back to you."[1]
>
> — SEATTLE BELLY DANCER DELILAH FLYNN DEFINING THE BELLY DANCER

I was instantly attracted to "leveling," moving my body higher and lower. For me, this meant dancing on the balls of the feet. I didn't know I was doing a specific technique. It simply felt natural to me as I and the other handful of students traveled across the floor with arms extended in the air. "That's more challenging," my petite instructor called out. We may have known each other for twenty-six minutes, but her wide smile and eyes said she was proud of me. In that instant, I realized that I forgot to have fear: fear of showing my body, of not hiding my arm in any shell. I inadvertently unlocked the level of confidence within my body.

Two decades into my life and I had only just begun clicking my body into place. Within that first year of physical leveling, wheeling my hips in place, and rotating my shoulders with veil work, I witnessed my body remembering itself from Day 1. This represented a new kind of Day 1, a rebirth. The more repetition that was introduced to my right side, the more it felt whole, something I couldn't know it as being. At one point, hip circling was more fluid on my weaker side and nearly forgotten on my stronger side; my left hip jumped from the circling technique to lifting outward, finding its hip kick instead.

> "Different Fabrics flow differently."
>
> — FLYNN DESCRIBING THE VEIL

During my rebirth phase, I constantly explored the feather that my right side had become: my arthritic-like strained fingers could no longer stay still; they stretched turning doorknobs, grasping pens, and learned to branch out across the keyboard. My wrist, constantly in extension, relaxed, allowing my thumb to reach each fingertip while warming up for dance.

But to enter a new phase also means that other phases will follow. Over time, the feather of my right side experienced being a sticky weight that required more energy to move. To avoid dwelling on the struggle, I turned to the Post-Its on my mirror and created nonfiction essays and poetry about dance. This was the newest creative phase under dance. And this third phase turned into a dormant dance phase.

As a dancer switches out veils, the type of fabric affects the flow of the movement. These phases I evolved into and out, and still evolve with, can either hold little or no weight to them. My physical struggles tend to be chiffon heavy, while the transition from dance into writing flows like silk satin. There are ebb and flow in my nondancing sequence.

> "What we have is a demonstration of the condensed value of creative experience- something beautiful out of a lot of outside pressure."
>
> — FLYNN EXPLAINING THE HIP SHIMMY

To still have the urge as an adult to hide my arm in its shell reinforces not only the outside pressure that says I have to hide what is different, but it also says that it's ugly. But no movement can truly be ugly. It's a reflection of being healthy and truthful. Rotating my right shoulder might be sticky, my fingers may tense up while kneading the air through extended arm, but that does not equate to being ugly from other dancers who simply need to warm up their bodies. We are all nearly immobile at some point. This is really a continuation of finding what phase, what kind of veil, is meant to be worked within the moment.

Each forefinger and thumb pinches my chiffon veil as I let it hang a few inches from the floor behind me. With veil in place, my left-hand rests on my head as I wave the other side of the veil forward and back with my right forearm like a matador. Quite the graceful southpaw writer, swinging her right side forward. The waves gradually gain fluidity over time. The irony behind this is through veil work; it gives my arm permission to unveil.

> "What we're born with is a body to move and express and feel, be in our right brain, be in our bodies."

After one of my many dormant dance phases, I finally experienced what dancing in and with the moment itself felt like. Without rehearsing at an outside venue for a charity event, my toes had to learn what balancing on small mounds of dirt felt like during the performance. More often than not, it was an intrusive push into my physical roots. The wind was our unexpected guest as the veil widened its waves through the air. Being actively conscious of these sensations introduced another beginning, another Day one. My right brain showed my right side that continuously moving in the moment reduces its fight-or-flight response in its tense muscles. This was a new approach for my body to recognize itself again. I "leveled" beyond just engaging in something that felt natural and found a way to switch my nervous system around.

Flynn believes that no one can write about dance or put words to it; one has to see it to understand its process. As I've experienced from under the tent of that charity event, I agree with one perspective. Yet, as someone who still needed to learn to be a southpaw from an early age, writing about how movement continually brings me back to my whole body, especially through the naval of belly dance, feels as natural to me as leveling. Writing about dance is leveling. I thirst for the left-brain structure to see the evolution under movements across the page. When I write to record my dance experiences, I immortalize my present relationship with courage and creativity.

---

1. All quotes are from an interview with Delilah Flynn.
   Delilah's Belly Dance Workshop [Volumes I, II, III]. Directed by Delilah Flynn and Steven Flynn. Visionary Dance Productions, 1990. Film.

PROPAGANDA ON POINTE: PARIS AND "THE RED DETACHMENT OF WOMEN"

TRACY HARRIS

I REACHED BAT MITZVAH AGE IN THE EARLY 1970S. STILL, WHILE THE other Jewish kids in my seventh-grade class were busy memorizing long passages of Hebrew text and planning the elaborate parties that would celebrate their attainment of Jewish adulthood, I was busy wondering what it felt like to believe in God. My parents were nonconformists in matters of religion, even for the liberal suburbs of Boston where I grew up. They told me religions were pretty much stories people devised to answer impossible questions. I'd be better off learning to think for myself. This was sort of OK, and in any event, if I wanted to be religious, Judaism was not the religion I would have picked. If it had been up to me, I'd have chosen to be Catholic.

It wasn't just because I wanted a Christmas tree or to wear the plaid skirts and navy blue sweaters required for girls at my town's two parochial schools. Bat mitzvah parties notwithstanding, the Jewish experience seemed focused on persecution and suffering. Being Catholic, from my outsider's perspective, was like belonging to the coolest sorority. Judaism had no matching outfits or magical transformations or adorable baby lying in a manger. Baby Moses adrift in the swampy Nile? Not even close. I'd moreover been raised to reject the day to day practice of my ancestors' religion. Hebrew prayers were guttural and embarrassing to pronounce. Biblical prohibitions on eating pork or mixing meat and dairy had no relevance in the modern, hygienic world. Jewish services, I knew from attending my cousins' bar mitzvahs, were long and tedious.

The Catholics, I knew from attending mass with my friend Maribeth, had you in and out in 45 minutes. Post-Vatican II Catholics said their prayers in English. Mass also involved a lot of engaging ecclesiastical activity: kneeling, receiving Communion, making dramatic gestures like the sign of the cross. Forehead, heart, left shoulder, right shoulder. In the pews with Maribeth and her family, I'd cross myself eagerly and gaze longingly at the altar, where according to my vague understanding, the wine and wafer were turning into God. Unfortunately, transubstantiation occurred only for Catholics; communion, Maribeth's mother gently explained, was not for me.

Despite being denied the Holy Eucharist, I appreciated Catholicism's blend of mystery and clarity. Especially the clarity. I loved that there were specific rules, e.g., attend mass every Sunday unless you went on Saturday afternoon, as I typically did with Maribeth. I loved that there were specific types of sins, mortal and venial. I loved that there were specific prayers, the Our Fathers and Hail Marys, that you could say to atone for committing those sins. And I loved the straightforward belief that following the rules and saying the prayers was all you had to do to get into heaven.

There was no religious clarity in Judaism, at least as interpreted by my family. Take cheeseburgers, which are supposedly forbidden under Jewish dietary laws. My immediate family ate them where- and whenever we wanted. My aunts, uncles, and cousins would eat cheeseburgers in restaurants or even at our house but not in their own homes. My grandmother would *never* eat a cheeseburger under any circumstances, and in fact, barely ate anything my mother cooked, even if it officially fell within the rules. Turns out our dishes were religiously tainted, which was merely a symptom of the larger problem, that my parents believed in nothing. Not in heaven and hell, certainly not in keeping kosher, and not in miracles or messiahs or going through the motions of a belief system that seemed pointless to them, not even to please my father's mother.

Belief didn't matter, my parents assured me. You could be a good person without belief. But that didn't mean we weren't Jewish, as Jewish as our more observant relatives. Hitler would have killed us all regardless of whether we kept kosher or could recite the prayers. It was, to say the least, confusing.

My teenaged religious covetousness ended more than forty years ago, but I still get a little wistful when I think about saint names or Holy Days of Obligation. I still love singing Christmas carols, which I learned largely from my father, who loved music and happened to attend a Jesuit university for graduate school. I can still rattle off a "Hail Mary" and an "Our Father." And I can sing the entire score of the rock-opera Jesus Christ Superstar from memory, start to finish.

JC Superstar was a pop music phenomenon back in the early 1970s. It seemed only natural that Maribeth and I would decide to mount our own production. We never actually performed for an audience, but along with my sister, cousin, and a group of neighborhood friends, we spent two summers singing and dancing along to the records. My 10-year-old cousin Alison had the best voice, and she shined in the one female role, a very blonde and very dramatic Mary Magdalene. Maribeth, the tallest and the one practicing Catholic in our group, was Jesus. I played all the bad guys—King Herod, Pontius Pilate, Judas.

I can still sing the whole opera, not just my solo numbers, but the entire score, straight through. I assume I've remembered the words because of all the months spent "rehearsing," but in truth, the pumped-up retelling of Christ's last week on earth struck more than musical chords. JCS became popular right at the time my Jewish friends were having their bat mitzvahs. My parents had blocked my access to that faith; I'd already been tiptoeing at the portals of Catholicism. Superstar became another passageway through which I'd try to enter the company of believers.

I never developed anything approaching actual faith, but I gave it my best effort. When I wasn't rehearsing JCS on the porch, I was in my room furtively reading the Gospels. If I got bored with Matthew, Mark, Luke, and John, I'd page through our family's book of world religions. And on Saturday afternoons, I made sure Maribeth and I were hanging out at her house, not mine, so that when 4:30 rolled around, her parents would have to invite me along to church. Those summers were the closest I came to becoming part of the Christian world. That I memorized an entire rock opera in the process was just a bonus.

Most Americans have not heard of another work that ranks high on my list of beloved musical productions, a Chinese ballet called "The Red Detachment of Women." RDW (the 1970 film version) is 105 glorious minutes of propaganda produced during the most tumultuous time in modern Chinese history, the Great Proletariat Cultural Revolution. Propaganda campaigns had been a staple of Communist rule from the moment Mao took power in 1949. Throughout China, posters, loudspeakers, radio broadcasts, and films exhorted the masses to show their revolutionary fervor and loyalty to the regime, sometimes by killing flies, sometimes by making steel in backyard furnaces. "Let a hundred flowers bloom!" "Learn from Lei Feng! (a revolutionary hero)" "Have fewer children, raise more pigs!" In Mao's China, the media and the arts served the revolution, and the ever-changing series of political campaigns formed an integral part of the fabric of life.

But during the Cultural Revolution, Maoist fervor spun out of control. It began in 1966, a manifestation of power struggles within the Communist party, and lasted until Mao died in 1976. During that time, millions of students and professionals were "sent down" to the countryside for work and re-education; people were subject to arbitrary accusations, public denunciations, and mob beatings; there were mass imprisonments and millions of deaths. All manner of communication was tightly controlled, including the arts. Mao's wife, former actress Jiang Qing, developed eight model dramas (two ballets, six operas) to promote "Mao Zedong Thought" during the Cultural Revolution. These were the only entertainment allowed. The Red Detachment of Women, a full-length ballet, is the most renowned and enduring of these works.

I first saw RDW when I was in high school. It was the waning years of the Cultural Revolution, a few years after those JC Superstar summers, and a few years after Richard Nixon's historic visit to meet Chairman Mao. I worked as a leader at our town Parks and Rec summer program; my program supervisor was a recent college graduate named Roy. Roy was seven glamorous years older than I was. He was tall and blond and played keyboard in a rock band. Unlike the boys in my high school, he seemed to enjoy talking to me. He studied Chinese, which back in the 1970s made him seem intellectual in a sophisticated and singular way, a swoon-worthy complement to his surfer-boy good looks.

Roy and I became friends—platonic friends, despite my best efforts to the contrary. He taught me how to play racquetball. He took me for my first *cha siu bao* (Chinese steamed pork bun) in Boston's tiny Chinatown. And one day, he invited me to a screening of Chinese films put on by Harvard's East Asian Studies Center.

So, yes, my first viewing of The Red Detachment of Women was imbued with the passion of first love. But it was not just my arm occasionally brushing up against Roy's in the darkened theater that set my heart pounding. RDW is a stirring tale, depicted on film with bright colors, bold, emotional lighting, stirring music, and choreography mainly derived from classical western ballet and drawing on traditional Chinese opera and ethnic folk dances. I would go on to study Chinese politics and language and even write a graduate thesis on Mao's use of propaganda. Still, that day in the small, musty auditorium, on a remote corner of the Harvard campus, I was just a young girl falling in love with the idea of awakening my revolutionary consciousness. I was finding a home among a group of rosy-cheeked woman soldiers, who sported bayonets on their rifles and khaki-colored toe shoes on their feet.

As much as it is an ode to the glory of Mao Zedong Thought, RDW is at its heart a coming-of-age tale. The heroine, Wu Qinghua, is a young peasant woman enslaved to an evil landlord on Hainan Island during China's civil war of the 1930s. After being beaten and left for dead by her cruel and reactionary master, Wu is taken in by a local communist brigade who warmly welcome her to become part of their struggle. But before she can be a true revolutionary, Wu must learn that success is achieved only through collaborative action, not by acting selfishly to avenge individual grievances. It takes several pas de deux and dramatically staged corps de ballet numbers, but Wu Qinghua finally learns what it means to devote oneself to a larger cause and, in the process, to become part of the group.

Wu develops her class consciousness under the guidance of a handsome male commissar, whom she admires with only the purest of revolutionary feelings. The parallel between Wu's feelings for her commissar and my feelings for my handsome playground boss was lost on me as I watched that day, as enthralled by the film as I was by the fact that technically I was out on a date with Roy. In subsequent viewings of RDW, I would watch closely for any signs of romance between Wu Qinghua and Commissar Hong Changqing, but there is none. My desire to turn RDW into a Maoist rom-com was apparently just a reflection of my bourgeois mentality and perhaps the slightest projection of the teenage infatuation that led me to see the film in the first place.

But RDW is so much more than the tale of a young woman and her handsome male mentor. As a work of political propaganda, it is designed to convey a clear message. The more I studied Chinese history and Chinese propaganda, the more I could see that RDW is the form's epitome. That it manages to extol the virtues of Mao using the vocabulary of ballet, arguably the most traditional and elite form of western dance, makes RDW all the more bizarre and extraordinary.

As in any good piece of propaganda, in RDW, there is simply no question about who is good, who is bad, and with whom the audience's sympathies should lie. This clarity permeates the film—the lighting, the emotive music, the camera angles—but is especially apparent in the choreography. When a character first appears on stage, they stop for a *Liang Xiang*, a traditional stance or pose derived from Chinese opera and designed to give the audience a clear sense of the character's moral probity. Dance movements then reflect the character's true nature, from Hong Changqing's heroic leaps and spins to the stooped and awkward scurrying of the evil landlord and his henchmen. And of course, there is the crisp precision of the dancers who comprise the Red Detachment: improbably costumed in toe shoes and khaki military shorts; as upright in posture as they are in their devotion to Chairman Mao; and smiling with revolutionary zeal as they dance, always in perfect unison.

And that was the message of RDW: unity. A group of young women accept an outcast girl and allow her to become one of them. Yes, when Wu Qinghua dons the khaki uniform and takes her place in line, she's giving her all for the Great Helmsman (Mao). But she's also a teenage girl getting the right clothes and being given a chance to join the cool group. The story is universal, except that in RDW, the cool group is not a high school clique or a snobby sorority but a Communist sisterhood united by a belief in a higher purpose. She was overthrowing the evil landlord, establishing a new China.

I first saw RDW back in high school. I had not wholly abandoned my adolescent search for some sort of belief system; ideally, one that involved stylish matching outfits and easy-to-execute weekly rituals. But by then, my quest for religious belonging had taken a back seat to my quest to be part of a high school social group, any group, cool or not. Wu Qinghua's success on both fronts was inspirational.

My friendship with Roy eventually faded, but I maintained my interest in China and Chinese films. The US formally recognized China in 1979; by then, I was in college studying Chinese and would continue to do so in graduate school. My interest in China never became part of my professional life, but it was always a part of me. I have taken Chinese classes on and off for years, and I go to Chinese films or dance performances whenever available.

China meanwhile retreated from the excesses of socialism and Maoist propaganda campaigns and traveled quite a way down the once-scorned "capitalist road." Over the years, Chinese society became more open; artists, including filmmakers, could create more nuanced works, which were no longer required to extol the virtues of

Chairman Mao. As China moved forward, I assumed that RDW had been left behind: this quaint and somewhat troubling reminder of a time when political ideals could be expressed through the gleam in a dancer's eye and the vigorous angle at which she tilted her bayonet while performing her piqué turns.

But ten years ago, as I was planning a trip to Paris, I was stunned to discover that the National Ballet of China—which I never knew existed—would be performing RDW at the Paris Opera House during the week my friends and I planned to visit.

"It's one of the ballets from the Cultural Revolution," I explained when I first suggested we get tickets. I realized that it wasn't an inducement for most people. But we were traveling to celebrate my 50th birthday, and as I was the first among these friends to turn 50, I was entitled to a bit of indulgence. Plus, the serendipity was undeniable. It had never occurred to me that RDW was ever performed live, much less that decades after that afternoon in the Harvard auditorium, I'd be able to see it at, of all places, the Paris Opera. On my birthday! It was as if everything I loved in life was coming together for that one moment.

"It's about this peasant girl who joins an all-female group of revolutionary soldiers," I continued—no more preposterous than a ballet about good and evil swans when you think about it.

"I don't mind going by myself," I went on, "but really, it's fantastic. It's like all this propaganda, *but it's a ballet!*"

Even as I made my pitch, I could hear how strange it sounded. In the end, it was perhaps my own propagandistic powers of persuasion that convinced my friends to sign on for the performance.

A few months later, I was seated in Center Orchestra, clutching my armrests as the dancers leaped across the stage from the left and the right, crisscrossing each other in a seemingly infinite stream of grand jetés. It's the choreographic climax of RDW, representing the Red Detachment's final advance upon the enemy forces. As stunning as this moment is on film, nothing can compare to seeing it live. My mouth hung open as I watched the precision and grace, and strength of the dancers. My heart pounded each time a toe-shoe hit the stage.

After the synchronized grand jetés, things wrap up quickly.

Commissar Hong dies in a blaze of proletariat glory, tied to a banyan tree and burned alive, using his last breath to denounce the evil landlords and praise the glory of Mao and the people's revolution as the *Internationale* sounds in the background. Wu Qinghua, inspired by Commissar Hong's sacrificing his own life for the greater good, leads the Red Detachment to storm the enemy's hideout and defeat the landlord's forces. An inspirational picture of Mao is projected onto a scrim behind the stage. Long live the revolutionary spirit of the people. And curtain.

"I'm so glad I sat down here with you," my friend Emily beamed. Three of our group had not wanted to pay for orchestra seats and were way up in one of the balconies. I learned later that they had fallen asleep during the performance. I felt a little guilty but not surprised.

"I mean, I didn't really get it," Emily continued, "but you were so excited!"

Excited? I was in a daze. Emily had had the presence of mind to whip out her phone and take some pictures as the performers were taking their bows. We were so close to the stage that you could actually see their faces, although, snapped quickly in the post-show frenzy, the images were a little blurred. Still, splurging on perfect seats for RDW had totally been worth it.

Meanwhile, the friends who'd sat up in the rafters were making their slow way down to the main lobby. Turned out they'd bought a copy of the full program, the one that costs 20 Euro or whatever that I would never have bought for myself. And over the next day or two in Paris, all five of my friends signed the program and then surprised me with it on the last day—the best birthday gift ever. I don't know who had it stashed under her coat that night as we headed back out into the cold and walked to a fabulous restaurant where we ate dinner and drank Kir royales and wine until well after midnight.

My husband, Will, had not been able to travel with me that winter; he was teaching and couldn't take time off. He would have indulged my quirky choice of entertainment; as my husband, he's somewhat obligated, and he's usually a good sport. As it turned out, however, seeing this peerless ballet celebrating Mao through the lens of female solidarity was even more magical with a group of women as my companions.

More than magical. It was one of the best nights of my life.

It wasn't just the city or the ballet or the late-night champagne. That night in Paris with a group of friends who, truth be told, are all better friends with each other than they are with me, I belonged. It was like those summers during junior high when rehearsing Jesus Christ Superstar was the perfect release from my anxiety about not belonging to my friends' Christian world or to the world of practicing Judaism. That night in Paris, a group of casual friends—who were in no way obligated to indulge my birthday wishes but who'd had the means and interest to travel with me—made me feel welcomed and treasured and part of the group in a way that I usually did not. They shared my love of Paris, and even though it put some of them to sleep, they shared my love of Chinese propaganda for one night.

That moment of belonging was a chimera. I'm still in touch with the group, but we're not really good friends. It's actually depressing when I see them because I feel their connection with each other and know I'm not included. Similarly, sometime after our second summer of rehearsing Jesus Christ Superstar, Maribeth dropped me. She had become good friends with another girl on our street, another Jewish girl who, as I recall, did not invite me to her bat mitzvah. The three of us walked to junior high together for a while until the day Maribeth and Janet said, "Tracy, we want to be frank with you." I was dumped; by Jesus. My father gave me a ride to school for the rest of the year.

A few years after the trip to Paris, I made my first trip to China. I was surprised to learn that many older people there feel nostalgia for the Cultural Revolution.

"My mother says these days all the young people want is money," my thirty-something tour guide told me. "When she was young, she had to work in the countryside. The conditions were hard, but she remembers the good times with her friends. And she thought they were doing something more important than worrying about their careers."

I came to realize that my tour guide's mother was not alone in seeing the upside of what was inarguably a time of brutality and enforced orthodoxy. I asked the guides in each city I visited. They confirmed that despite the hardships, for many Chinese, the Maoist era and even the Cultural Revolution continue to represent an idealistic time, when their society was united for a nobler purpose than today's capitalistic careerism.

This longing to be part of a group working toward a utopian ideal begins to explain, perhaps, why one can still find images from the old-style propaganda posters for sale all over China and why RDW remains part of the repertoire of the national ballet. It might also explain why, although I ended up too cynical and independent to sign on to any organized belief system, the idea that I could be one of the (Jewish) tribe or a member of the (Christian) flock retains its appeal. And why, like my near-perfect recall of Jesus Christ Superstar, my passion for The Red Detachment of Women has lasted for more than 40 years.

The Russians introduced ballet to China, and I love the cross-cultural wackiness that comes from making this aristocratic art form fit Mao's proletarian worldview. I love the paradox of Mao's regime finally purging China of foot-binding, only to create their greatest piece of propaganda using an art form that requires women to dance in hard, excruciatingly painful shoes. I love the meticulousness of Jiang Qing's choreography. She developed the revolutionary ballets, banning standard moves like partnered lifts because they represented Western heterosexual chivalry and thus ran counter to Mao Zedong Thought.

But most of all, I love RDW because despite the repression and brutality Chinese propaganda has engendered, there is something so pure about its vision. The Chinese Communist Party, like organized religion, is hardly a perfect institutional vessel. Still, it offers up an ideal of commitment, and unity like a crusty, jagged oyster shell offers up a glistening pearl. As much as I value intellectual and moral autonomy, when I watch RDW, I am transfixed by its depiction of belonging. By the bayonets and the pirouettes. By the kindness and the courage of the soldiers. By the faith that makes it possible to give yourself up to a group, to cast aside your individual doubts and differences, to don the uniform, to take the pledge, to stand toe to pointed toe alongside your rosy-cheeked sisters-in-arms and step forward in perfect unison toward one shared and glistening future.

THERE WILL BE BLOOD

SM LINDBERG

As I changed into my gym clothes, I faced the metal locker in front of me with my eyes closed tight and tried to undress and redress as quickly as possible. My morphing teenage body embarrassed me, especially in the presence of other people. I wore a loose t-shirt, white shorts with a black fleur-de-lis design and an elastic waist, and nondescript athletic shoes -- high fashion. I carefully secured my thick glasses with a purple band and pulled my long, brown hair into a messy loop at the back of my head.

The girls at tryouts were classmates, not friends; I didn't have many of those. Some had picked on me during regular school days. Others ignored me for the most part; I preferred this.

We went through organized warm-ups. Twenty or so girls lunged forward, raising our hands above our heads. We ran laps. We twisted, one foot crossed in front of the other, our way across the floor. The coaches explained there would be two volleyball teams formed, intermediate and advanced, which roughly translated to seventh and eighth grades.

We did drills: digs, sets, blocks, and spikes. The coach sent balls soaring my way, and I tried to dig as many balls as possible. I dived and slid on my knee pads, my arms flexed out to meet the ball just before it hit the floor. I rolled over my shoulder, as the coaches had shown us, to bounce back into form. I blocked a few balls at the net, imitating some of the more experienced girls.

Setting was not my forte.

I knew I could improve on spiking; I liked the idea the word projected. I imagined a metal ball with medieval spikes careening into the floor, avoiding the outstretched arms of opposing players.

Finally, we practiced serving. One by one, we rotated on the court to play a scrimmage. When it was my turn, my serve broke just over the net and nosedived, bouncing untouched to the floor. My team shouted encouragement.

"Yeah! Just like that!"

"Ace!"

"Like a bomb!"

When I did the same thing three more times, I saw one of the coaches smile and nod.

"Go ahead and rotate, girls, so we can see the rest of your serves."

E, who rarely spoke to me though we had most classes together, clapped me on the shoulder as we rotated.

"Good job."

My cheeks burned.

"Thanks."

The coaches called us individually to review. The coaches praised my digs and serves.

"I know this is your first year," one coach said, "But we are going to try you on the advanced team with a serve like that."

Thrilled, I picked out my number (I wanted Elway's 7, but settled for Favre's 4 -- he led the Packers to a Super Bowl a few months later). The advanced team had brand new uniforms. The shirts, white with black and red splashes, were nice. But the black spanks were horrifying to a group of teen girls. Our shirts would barely reach the hem. I imagined having my period during a game and having to wear a pad. Wouldn't it show?

"Do we really have to wear these?" someone asked, spinning a pair on one finger, as we eyed the intermediate team's kit. They had regular gym shorts.

"Better get used to them," a coach said with a grin. "See you all at practice. Make sure you wash those uniforms before wearing."

We returned to the changing room. My new teammates kindly expressed congratulations to me, and I to them. As I began to change, I realized that my shorts were no longer white; they were streaked with red. Embarrassed, my face hot, I quickly ran to the toilet stall. Our school never had pads in stock, despite having dispensers. I made do with a wad of toilet paper. When I emerged, I stared at the concrete floor and walked back to my locker, ashamed of my body. What must everyone else be thinking about me? What an idiot; I didn't even notice! And there was no doubt everyone else had seen my shorts change color.

"Hey," someone said as I pulled on my jeans. "We've all been there. We're all girls."

"Do you need anything?" someone else added.

Surprised, I glanced up.

"No, but thank you."

Several girls wore rueful smiles.

"Damn periods," another girl said.

We all laughed, each imagining our past mortifying bloody moments in camaraderie.

NURSE'S CAP

LINDA MILLER

MY MOTHER'S OLD NURSING CAP LOOKS LIKE AN UPSIDE-DOWN SNOW-cone cup nestled behind a three-inch wall of starched white cotton. Not that I'd ever do this, but I swear it'd drift away on a fair wind should I toss it into the drink. It's sturdy and wide at the bottom, and the peak provides ample sail. Stuart Little might climb aboard, find it seaworthy and push off, standing steady at the helm.

Its size and shape make me wonder how it stayed in place, considering all the bending, lifting, sheet-changing, and feeding she must have provided in the hospital. But then I see my answer. Bobby pins. The two she used to secure it to the top of her head are slipped onto the back and pry open a deep stash of memories. When I was a child, I'd watch her standing in front of a mirror with two pins stuck between her teeth. She'd spin strands of hair around her fingers and then flatten them onto the side of her head, just below the temple. Then she'd pluck both pins from her lips to slide over the top of the future curl, making a perfect X.

The cap--and the pins-- form a dynamic duo of tribute to my Mom, who stopped nursing in the late 50s. I suspect she wrapped her cap in the same hardened plastic bag that shelters it now. She stored it on the top shelf of her bedroom closet, where it sat for decades, untouched until she died in 2001. That's when her cap came to live with me. Of Mom's many layers, the cap connects to an early one formed during the war years, when she faced black mornings at 5 a.m. to grab the bus for her 7 a.m. shift in Allentown. The cap is my mother at her grittiest. The cap is Mom before me.

Now I'm in my mid-60s, the throttle back decade when it comes to stuff. I must stare down the belongings I've collected during my lifetime and determine which objects bring me joy, the new litmus test for what stays and what goes. I cast joy-seeking eyes on old photos, dishes, dusty vases, candlesticks, and plates. Mom's cap makes me second guess everything because it sits at the fault line of joy and old memories, respect, and obligation. Should I memorialize it on a shelf? Throw it out? Donate? Where? Someday soon, I'll need to make a decision. Or not. If I'm lucky enough to wait it out another 15-20 years, my minimalist daughter will cut the cord.

But that seems cowardly, doesn't it? Putting things off is no way to honor my mother. When faced with dilemmas---health or otherwise —she'd always say, "Handle it. Handle it."

Lucky for me, another nurse comes to the rescue.

I reconnect with Mary, one of my best friends from high school. During one late-night phone call, we cover lots of ground in our conversation, exchanging details of Mary's divorce and my husband's latest trip to the ER. I offhandedly mention how all the nurses look so very different from how my mother appeared in her graduation photos.

"I remember a doctor I knew in the old days who said everything changed when nurses stopped wearing their caps," Mary begins. "Funny, I can't find mine. Must have lost it along the way."

"I still have my Mom's."

"Really? She went to Allentown for training, didn't she?"

"Yea. Why?"

"Well....that means her cap would be the same as mine."

"The same? I don't follow."

Mary tells me that back in the day, each nursing school designed its own cap for graduates and student nurses, a tradition I discover began at Bellevue Hospital School of Nursing back in 1874. An internet search reveals a wide variety of styles, some more fashion-forward than others. They range from Bellevue's soft, gauzy bonnet to caps that look like upended flower pots. While a few have frills, others go hard and severe, with peaks like teepees. Short, squat, tall, narrow, striped. My favorite is the slim, aerodynamic lines of the Bryn Mawr cap. It looks like an upside-down Nike swoosh. No matter the style, a nurse's cap becomes her resume and represents high-toned respectability, a solid work ethic, and the call to serve.

"Well, maybe you'd like my Mom's cap," I suggest. "I really don't know what to do with it, and I know she'd be thrilled to know that you'd be hanging on to it."

I hear her take a big breath of air on the other side of the phone. She's excited, I can tell.

"YES! I'd love it." Even after decades apart, I know Mary's delight meter and how she sounds when she's happy. Her voice registers higher and louder, and there's no doubting her appreciation.

This whole sisterhood of the traveling cap gets me thinking about Mom's life as a nurse and mother. I believe her nurses' training added a steely edge to her comforting core, and what she learned and observed during her career spilled over into her life with me. Her teachings, her warnings, her instructions took seed decades ago and still send up shoots when everyday life rains down upon me.

Like when I put on clean sheets, fresh off the clothesline. After the fitted sheet's in place, I float the sweet-smelling flat sheet over top. Once it gets tucked in along the foot of the bed, I move to the side to start the first of two slick hospital corners. It's a weekly homage to my mother, who showed me the ropes way back in the 60s when I was in junior high and had zero interest in sheets or chores of any kind.

"Linda. C'mere. I want to show you something," she yells from my bedroom.

Obligingly, I trudge to the back of the house. My legs drag because enlightenment bores me today.

"This is how you make a hospital corner. You should know how to do this."

Big sigh. Big eye roll.

"Oh, yea." My arms cross in front of my chest.

She ignores me and begins the tutorial.

"Once you tuck in this top sheet at the bottom, you go to the corner and pick up this extra stuff hanging over."

"Ahh. Ya."

"And then you tuck in the part that's still hanging down. Like this."

"Ahh. Ya."

"And then you bring this part down again and tuck it in. And that's a hospital corner. See?

"Ahh. Ya. Can I go?"

Now, my corners are top-notch. They finish up sharp and crisp and make the whole bed look like it's at attention, waiting patiently to go on duty. I like that the beds in my house mean business, and I can thank my mother for that.

During my know-it-all teen years, Mom provided a dermatology lecture that changed me for life. It started with a small, neon yellow pimple that flourished in the crevice alongside my nose. Its bright yellow peak flashed its presence to anyone approaching me head-on, a beauty dilemma requiring decisive action. I march into the bathroom, stand in front of the mirror, and plan my mode of attack. Leaning in, surveying, my fingers slowly find their target and begin to squeeze.

"DON'T DO THAT!" Mom cries like I'm sticking a pair of scissors into my eye. Had I known she was in the vicinity cleaning, I'd have shut the door.

"Whaaaaat?"

"Don't ever pick at a pimple around your nose," she says, pointing, like a furious Uncle Sam. "Don't you know it's called the triangle of death?"

"Triangle of DEATH? You're making that up," I chuckle as I step away from the mirror.

Her reliably sunny face turns dark and angry. "If germs get in there, it's a straight path to your brain! Don't EVER (big pointing gestures now) pick at a pimple around your nose. You don't want to get an infection!"

The infamous triangle of death incident stays with me FOREVER, and when pinpoints of red dare to show anywhere near the center of my face, I respect the triangle and stay far away.

Mom's nursing skills—and her stash of scary medical equipment--

also made my brother and me fair game for procedures better left undescribed or revisited. Like, um... enemas, which at the time seemed like gastro-intestinal waterboarding.

After a bout of strep throat or the flu and we were down for a week, Mom supplemented the antibiotics with the dreaded, "C'mon, we're going into the bathroom" summons. My abiding memories are of me sitting on the toilet, crying throughout the whole splashy assault. Rubber bags, tubing, water going places it really didn't belong. I never heard other kids talk about this indignity happening in their homes. Her previous life as a nurse, I knew, was to blame.

As my brother and I got older—and less sick--Mom assigned herself elsewhere. By the time I left for college, my grandmother, Mom's mother, suffered a heart attack. After discharge from the hospital, she recuperated in my recently vacated pink bedroom, and Mom took charge like she was back on the ward. No fussing. No fretting. Just action. Three years later, my grandmother suffered a stroke, and again, Mom stepped in to provide end-stage home care and remained at her side until she passed months later.

She was always on call. In the next two decades, she cared for her mother-in-law with breast cancer and my father's aunt, who needed transitional care before moving into assisted living. When I broke a wrist and required surgery, pins, and plaster back in the late 90s, she traveled to my home each week for eight weeks to lend a hand.

I'm not a nurse, but I've observed one during a good portion of my life. I don't have her credentials, but I now do the work of a healer and helper as I travel along with my husband Steve on his Parkinson's journey. Most days, I believe she's bequeathed me her capable hand and compassionate touch.

In times of reflection, I listen for her voice, her good counsel, and then pat myself on the back for handling—her favorite word-- the latest health emergency. I replay episodes from my time at home: Mom placing a cool hand on my forehead checking for fever, Mom applying an ice pack to an ankle sprain, or Mom delivering a tray of tea and toast to my sickbed. Afterward, I breathe deep, push forward, and believe I can do whatever comes next. I become my mother, just without the cap.

ARTICLES OF FAITH

ELIZABETH TEMPLEMAN

THERE ARE THINGS I TAKE ON FAITH—FEWER, PERHAPS, THAN WHEN I was a child. Back then, I could conjure up the holy trinity and a platoon of saints to quell a fear or still a tremor of uncertainty. Now, to stem my disquieting thoughts, I take a breath and plunder inner reserves for solace.

What exactly do I believe? In what, or whom, do I have faith? I believe in this tired old earth. I struggle to sustain faith that humankind will right its most egregious wrongs and restrain its most absurd and dangerous impulses. I have faith in my family, those I love most, to be decent and good and to carry forward traditions of decency and goodness. I believe in scientific thinking, but I believe just as surely in its limitations—those of human fallibility: pride, deceit, foolishness.

I have faith in stories. I believe that life is a gift and that each life is special. I believe that we are responsible for being grateful for our lives and nurturing mind, body, and spirit. Those are some of the things I believe in, and they give me comfort. Though I am an optimist by nature, I think that my faith in goodness grounds my optimism.

When I was ten, Jesus Christ was as real to me as Ed Sullivan. I believed in Heaven and Hell and even Purgatory. There was another realm—a sketchier concept in our teaching—Limbo: a state of suspended innocence for unbaptized infants, whom I imagined as rather like tiny, flightless angels with buds where wings would be. I struggled with the notion that my God would discriminate, even in such a benign way, against those tiny babies, let alone allowing suffering and damnation for the less innocent. I wondered how he could—and why ever he would—keep my good friend, a Methodist, out of Heaven. Yet our Heaven was exclusively Catholic. I was endlessly curious about the folly of all those other churches.

Within our church, Saint Bernard's Catholic Church, our family's pew was to the altar's left and close to the vestibule. How that got determined remains a mystery to me. We would be meticulously dressed, thanks to my mother's care—our hats bobby-pinned to gleaming hair, and our white gloves and shining patent leather shoes —but nothing about our appearance or position ever seemed casual. Our parish included families of Italians (like us) and Irish, a few French, Greek, and Hungarian—mostly, I think, an immigrant population. Our dentist's extended family, fair-haired Irish or Scottish, were close to the center and to the right of us. Ahead of us were the flying saucer sisters, subject of great mirth for my younger sister and me. They were clearly well off, dressed in store-bought fashions and always those wide-rimmed, ribboned hats. Clustered at the front were a few ancient women, some with furs wrapped around their shoulders.

I desperately wanted to grow up to belong to Christ, to live in a convent—cloistered preferably—and to wear a white and black habit with beads and a crucifix around my waist. Because it seemed so hard to be good enough, and I surely knew temptation (for candy at lent, for toys my neighbors owned), I prayed for God to nudge me along that pathway when the time was right. I watched the movie about the miracle of Fatima and prayed for, or dreamed of (to the extent that such dreams were distinct from all those childish prayers), my own vision of The Virgin Mother, something to prove, undeniably—to my family and me, never mind the world at large—that I was worthy.

My beliefs sometimes overwhelmed me. Evenings I whispered rosaries to myself, pulling the beads along through my fingers, the Hail Marys a blur of syllables. I was often wrapped in an aura of my own blend of Catholicism and superstition. Probably I missed things happening outside the haze of that sweeping faith. No doubt, I made dumb mistakes and took bone-headed risks because I relied so heavily upon my beliefs.

Thirty years ago, as our relationship evolved, my husband and I seldom talked about faith, though we did share stories about our early experiences with religion. I think we may have intended to have some kind of conversation before we had kids, but it didn't quite happen. By then, we were preoccupied with demands of resourcefulness and practicality, in the whirl and intoxicating joy of creating a life for ourselves.

When our oldest was in university, out of the blue during one of our Sunday evening telephone conversations, she mentioned (not quite accusingly) that she was the only one among her university friends who'd never been in a church. I don't know how long that realization had been percolating, but our daughter is thoughtful, and things don't seem to tumble from her mouth unconsidered. This had likely weighed on her mind for a while.

In retrospect, I may have been the only one in the family, including our mother, on whom Catholicism had so deep a hold. My older sisters and brother made fun of me, relentlessly. To them, the church was just one more imposition on their freedom: one more demand of conformity for us (along with good grades, decent clothing, balanced meals).

When things came badly undone in our family, my mother left the church. I don't remember whether it was an abrupt or a gradual shift toward negligence. I don't know if my mother was a believer and the carelessness of our God just wore her down, or if her Catholicism was a vestige of her upbringing which came to yield too little reward for the trouble. What I do remember is that for years normal was being at church every Sunday morning, and usually other times during the week (for Catechism, Saturday baked bean dinners, kids' summer games, and holiday parties, and sometimes, holy-roller that I was, for private prayer). Church was central to our social and cultural life. And then, one day, it was not. Even on Sunday, or at Christmas or Easter, we didn't go there.

Somewhere in the midst of that rift, I experienced my own loss of faith.

It's odd how unclear my memory is, as though I had been enveloped in a cloud throughout the months or years of this change (among others). What I know is that for years I belonged in Saint Bernard's Church. I could enter at any time, dropping in a coin to light a votive candle, praying to the statue of Mary or Saint Anne, or sometimes to the Stations of the Cross lining the walls. The church was always open; I always had a familiar, safe, and comfortable place there until I didn't.

How could our church one day make me feel so blessed, and the next, fall right out of my life? I don't know how I filled the void. I only remember filling my days as most kids did—bike-riding, reading, playing softball, and delving into the intricacies of older-kid friendships.

The personal objects of my faith—tiny rosary beads in a small faded pink plastic egg (earned by flogging Christmas cards, mostly to our relatives), my ivory-colored plastic Virgin Mary, our wooden crèche with its porcelain figures, and a pewter set of rosary beads nestled in its oval locket—those still resonated, and do even now, with a gentle charm. They carry the warm memory of veneration, nothing more.

Later, my mother would talk about God. She was ninety-two and had been away from the church for more than forty years. I don't think, back when we were a Catholic family, and we ever really discussed God or our faith. It was surprising, even a little bit alarming when my mother brought it up. When she talked of death (her topic of choice for years), she'd speak of "going home" to be with her mother and brother.

Though she was relatively healthy and keen-minded right to the end, she sometimes seemed to inhabit a realm of faith that brought her more comfort than the world around her could do. While I can't imagine this, I do wonder if approaching death will also bring me back to faith. Should such an inconceivable thing come to pass, what would happen to my sense of logic—to the way I know the world?

Not long after my daughter mentioned that she'd never been in a church, which could surely be taken to be a shortcoming, our youngest son asked me if I believed in God. His question, without context or any warning at all, uttered as he backed out the kitchen door with a hockey stick under his arm, elicited a spontaneous but shockingly certain "No." Unlike his sister, he's always seemed quite able to speak without much—or any—conscious deliberation. I tried to tack on some thoughts about believing in lots of things, goodness, for example, but he was out the door before I was finished my salvage operation. I have no idea what prompted the exchange, and he'd lost interest in the conversation when I tried to renew it later.

Though we never really articulated it, I think we intended to raise children free of dogma or to grow up in the shadow of what seemed to us irrelevant belief. I know that I didn't want to imagine my kids preoccupied in the way that I indeed was—consumed by ideas and beliefs and apprehensions so far removed from the immediate, tangible world. But sometimes, I worry that the fears surrounding these kids—of environmental collapse, acts of war and terror, random crime—are so very much entrenched in this world that their grip will become intolerable. By comparison, those seem to fear of damnation or hellfire, too substantial, too much of this world. At other times I worry that what does seem to preoccupy them—their iPods and hoodies and shoes—are so trivial, so insubstantial, as to undermine their existence. By freeing them from religion, did we also free them from other, more sustaining kinds of faith? Have we circumscribed their world in our effort to open it?

In an article I once read torn from an old issue of MacLean's, that many teens of Western denominations are losing faith. According to Reginald Bibby, a sociologist from the University of Lethbridge, some teens are deeply devoted to their religions and those who don't believe at all. The fewest, however, believe moderately. The percentage of Christian teens is shrinking fastest. Bibby questioned how this change would affect our social stability, change our ethics and behavior as a society. Will teens find a moral compass, he wonders, to replace established religion?

Thinking back to my teen years, I don't remember how our Catholicism's residual effects affected my moral orientation. I don't remember people from our church as being particularly kind or, indeed, unduly constrained by ethical considerations. Most families in our town were church-goers, and everyone generally knew everyone else's affiliation. This seemed part of the public domain. And although I rarely felt threatened in our schools and on our streets, I do remember bullying, locker break-ins, graffiti, drunkenness, and sometimes violence. It doesn't seem much different than what our kids have been exposed to in their teen years.

Trying to itemize what, exactly, established faith contributed to my early years, this is what I come up with: a sense of romance and awe; a community; a reverence for something greater than our own lives; fear, guilt, and the occasional nightmare; discipline and sacrifice; baked bean dinners and scorched hot chocolate; sometimes, a sense of comfort and safety. If that's the stuff of religion, then I wonder how our kids have compensated in their own growing up.

Because indeed they have. I find myself with one more thing to believe in: that individuals, or those blessed with ordinary circumstances, will find what they need in life. Discipline and sacrifice, for example, can be found, of all unlikely places, in a hockey rink or soccer field. A sense of romance and mystery abounds in the worlds created by L.M. Montgomery and R.K. Rawling, among others. Reverence for what is greater? What better than an introduction to the wonders of the world just outside the door: hummingbirds, for example, or bats. Even rose hips. And surely there's no better inspiration for fear and awe than forest fires.

Maybe, if they look for it, Bibby and his successors will find that a good life, lived ethically, with meaning and a keen awareness of one's surroundings, can be had without the dogma, the churches, or parishes.

Meanwhile, our daughter visits churches now, mostly in her travels, taking in the architectural riches and the complex history of those lofty structures. She may even choose, someday, to dance with their doctrines—just as I chose, years ago, to walk away.

THE RIGHT PLACE AT THE RIGHT TIME

DENISE THOMPSON-SLAUGHTER

WHILE WALKING ALONG THE LEVEE OF THE DELAWARE RIVER ON THE Pennsylvania side, just across from Trenton in spring of 1996, I "received" the simple command: "SIT DOWN." Hearing voices? I had been under a lot of stress: I figured I must be losing it. I also didn't like the idea of getting orders, but I warily looked around and noticed there was actually a bench nearby. Either it was new, or I'd never really noticed it before.

I've since read that the "New York Subway Hero," Wesley Autrey, Sr., heard a voice in 2007, just before he dove onto the subway tracks to save the life of an unknown man who had fallen during an episode of epilepsy. Mr. Autrey's voice said, "Go save that life; don't worry about your own; don't worry about your daughters." So he did. Fortunately, my faith was not tested so hard: sitting is pretty easy for me. So when the voice told me to sit, I sat. Seemed pretty harmless.

"Okay," I thought, " but what am I waiting for?" I looked around. A movement down the bank, maybe fifty yards to my right, caught my eye. A man was standing on the edge of the lowest retaining wall, looking into the swirling water that the spring rains had brought down from the mountains of the Delaware River Water Gap, to splash against the banks of the city and the pylons of the bridge. This is the bridge with giant block letters that read "Trenton Makes, The World

Takes"—Trenton's claim to a glorious industrial past that was now nothing but a ghost of prosperity. The man was well dressed in slacks and a standard white business shirt, and he looked to be young—in his twenties, I thought. I wondered what on earth he was doing. It was not easy to clamber down the steep and uneven stone levee; the ledge on which he stood was only about six inches wide. He just stood there. I had no other notions of what I was supposed to do, so I just sat. I did wonder if he was thinking of jumping, but I had no proof of that. Maybe he was thinking whether it would be a good fishing spot? But he certainly wasn't dressed for fishing or for the rough climb. He looked up at me, realized I was watching, and looked away. I continued to sit; he continued to stand, staring at the water below. The longer I sat there, the more convinced I was that he was thinking of jumping and was just waiting for me to leave. At certain times of the year, it would be a painful, but probably not a fatal jump; but in spring, there were hidden rocks and whirlpools and a lot of rushing water. The bridge, a more logical jumping place, was filled with traffic, as were the other two bridges in the afternoon—and they had either guards to prevent heavy vehicles from crossing or, on the Jersey side of Route 1, toll-collectors.

The man looked up at me periodically to see if I was still there, and I could almost feel his mounting annoyance. A little while later, for no reason I can convey, I found myself singing "Amazing Grace." (Most remarkable is that my singing didn't drive the poor man over the edge!) I just sat on that bench and sang three rousing verses of "Amazing Grace," feeling profoundly silly and embarrassed and glad no other hikers were coming along. Still, the man did not move, except to glance up at me every ten minutes or so and sometimes to pace a few feet on the narrow ledge. I must have been there an hour when, finally, he clamored up the steep stone on all fours and went over the levee to his expensive sports car that was, I now saw, parked at the bottom of the bank. He got in the car and made as if he would drive away. He started the car, then turned the engine off. He sat. He looked at me. He sat. He got out of the car and opened his trunk. He poked around in his trunk a bit, got back in the car, and sat.

"Oh, I get it," I thought. "You want me to think you've changed your mind, and you're leaving. Unh unh. I'm staying until you really leave." I suppose he thought I had a cell-phone, and he didn't want to be rescued. But I was one of the last people in America to get a cell-phone, and I only did so when I discovered one of my children had a life-threatening allergy.

Fifteen minutes later, with a final look of exasperation at me, he started his sporty car, gunned the engine, and took off. I watched him roar up to the main road and across the bridge to Trenton.

"You can be as angry as you like, buddy," I thought. "But I think I just saved your life."

As I walked back down the levee toward my own car at the other end, I felt so light and happy, as if I was walking with the unseen. Geese took off from the path and soared over the river, and I felt for a second that I was one of them. As I turned on the ignition, one of my favorite songs was playing on the radio. And when I went home and started dinner, I put a new Sting album on the CD-player. I heard for the first time, with trembling, "I Was Brought to My Senses," in which Sting writes about seeing the world in a new way, seeing all around him what was previously hidden "like a veil had been removed from before my eyes/For the first time I saw the work of heaven/in the line where the hills had been married to the sky." And he saw two birds rise from the river, "And where the two birds were flying/I swear I saw you and I."

A few months later, after I dropped my daughter off at half-day preschool, I headed for another of my favorite walking spots, the Delaware and Raritan Canal path. As I left the school, although I didn't see her, I found myself thinking of a woman who also had a daughter in the preschool and whose son had attended kindergarten with mine. Although we weren't that close, I had liked her from the first time I met her; and I knew that her family was under a lot of stress. I had picked up hints that they'd had a number of health and employment problems lately, and I suddenly felt very concerned for her and wished that I could help in some way. As I pulled in to park along the edge of the road where I customarily picked up the canal path, however, I tried to clear my mind for my usual "walking meditation."

Only a few minutes down the path, I saw someone bunched up under a tree by the path. At first, I thought maybe the person was sick or injured and that I should offer to help. As I got a little closer, I could hear sobs and wondered if the sufferer just wanted to be left alone. I paused, not knowing whether to approach or not and went one or two tentative steps nearer. She must have heard me then, because she looked up, and I was astonished to see the woman I had just been thinking about. Instinctively and without hesitation, I ran up, dropped to my knees, and hugged her. I wasn't sure how that would go over, but it turned out she was very grateful and cried on my shoulder. After a few minutes, she started to try to explain in broken sentences.

"Don't feel like you have to tell me anything," I said, "but I'll be glad to listen if you want to talk."

She collected herself and poured out all her family's latest problems. She had to decide whether to have potentially dangerous back surgery. She talked about her husband's lay-off from work, a child's learning disabilities, and school problems (an issue we shared) and their need to decide whether to move out of state or not for an offered but not-very-promising job. We walked and talked for forty-five minutes, and she told me that she thought God must have sent me because she was afraid that if she had tried to go home earlier, she would have rammed her car into a tree. For my part, I was glad to have been "sent," both for her and for me: I had been feeling particularly ineffective, earth-bound, and useless for the past few weeks. It gave me great joy to be able to be helpful with even such little free time and energy as I had in those days. It was a good reminder that sometimes "help" can consist of simply being in the right place at the right time.

Coincidence, you say? Maybe. Once I would have said so myself. But there are only so many bizarre coincidences one person can collect, and my coincidence cup overfloweth. Although I still look back on this in wonder and a sense of unease and have never talked about it to anyone, I have become a disbeliever in coincidence.

VISUAL ART GALLERY

Dance Me to the End of Love

Ann Marie Brown

Dancing Alone

Ann Marie Brown

Sisters of Mercy

Ann Marie Brown

White Iris in Light

Patricia Joynes

For Next Years Monarch

Martha Nance

Rhythm of the River

Martha Nance

Unblemished

Martha Nance

Remedios Cuba

Jeanne Julian

In Blue

Anthony Afairo Nze

Anna

Anthony Afairo Nze

Evening Beach
Anthony Afairo Nze

Summer in Anola

Anthony Afairo Nze

New Challenge

Ernst Perdriel

Resource 2020

Ernst Perdriel

Day Lights

Karen Starrett

Inner Music

Karen Starrett

Room to Grow

Karen Starrett

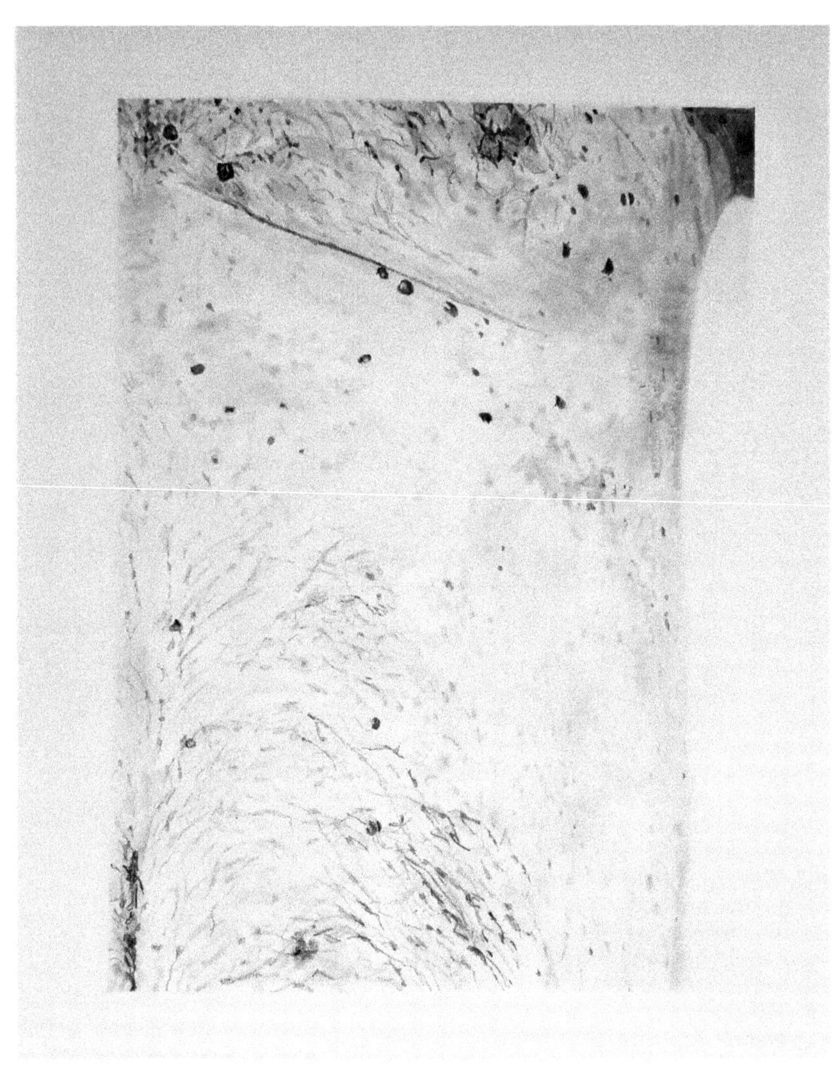

Selfie Left Chest

Morrie Warshawski

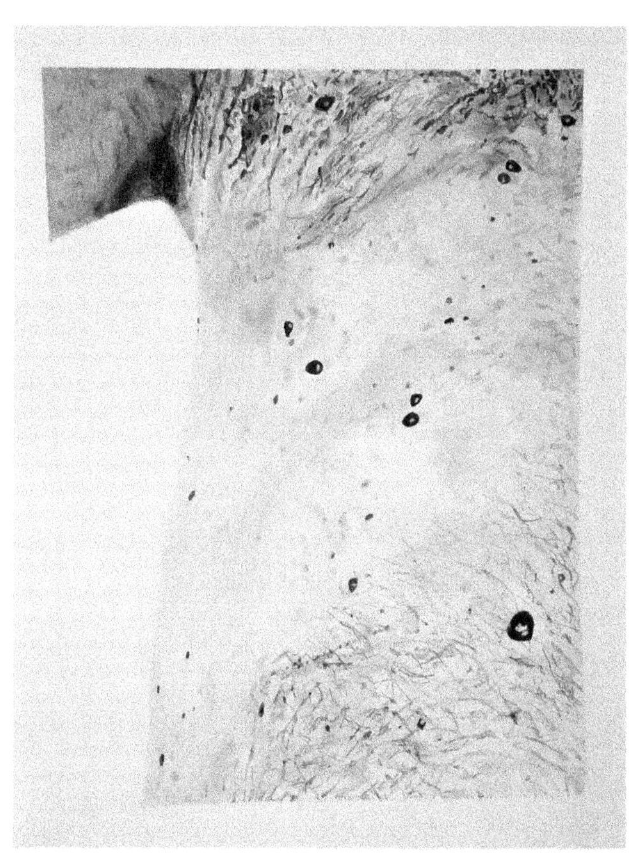

Selfie Right Chest

Morrie Warshawski

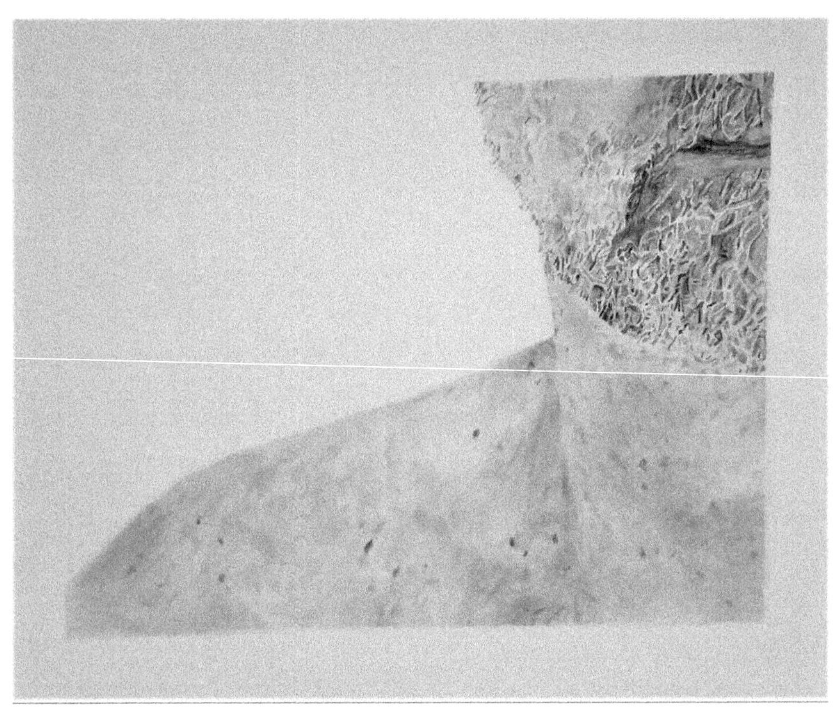

Selfie Right Chin

Morrie Warshawski

Always

Cynthia Yatchman

FICTION

MIRACLE

RAMONA GABAR

WHEN I TURNED SIX, MY MOTHER BOUGHT ME MY FIRST PAIR OF SHOES. They were green and stiff like wood logs, but to me, they were the most beautiful things I had ever seen.

Later on, it turned out that mom hadn't bought them: the volunteers from a charitable association had distributed hand-me-downs to people in our village. Even after I'd learned that the shoes had belonged to someone else, they still stroke me like the most beautiful things I had ever owned.

When we were kids, we used to run to the village's edge, where there were no more houses but only the sizable plain field, to play until late in the night. When the stars came out, we sat around in a circle, with our backs to each other and our feet facing out, watching the sky. The contest went: one day, who finds the most animal shapes; another, who finds the most shapes of plants; yet again, who finds the most shapes of objects. Manuel always called the theme of the day: he was the oldest and the only one going to school. Sometimes he would teach us the numbers by tracing them with a stick in the sand.

- Look, now you're ready for school, Mom said when she brought me the shoes. There were three more weeks. I went outside, I hid behind the tree in our backyard, and I cried. Paloma would stay at home, and I knew I was going to miss her.

Not long after that, uncle Ernesto came to let us know that daddy is not coming home ever again. He first told Mom in the corner of our yard, and then mom sat there, on her stool, and from a distance, I couldn't tell if she's upset or not. Then uncle Ernesto came inside, called Paloma and me, and told us precisely these words:

- Your father is not coming back.

Paloma watched my face to see my reaction so that she'd know what to do. For her sake, but also because we only saw daddy a few times a year, I didn't cry. I held her hand tightly, and I asked her if she wants us to go to the river and see who finds the most colorful pebble.

Mom called after me to take good care of Paloma, to make sure she doesn't go in, and from her voice, I realized she hadn't cried either, perhaps also not to scare Paloma.

The hum of cicadas filled the yard, and I loved to sit in the shadow of our house's wall, to close my eyes, and listen to the clamor. And then I heard my mother's voice coming out through the window like a rumble of thunder breaking the silence:

- Ernesto, I'm a single mom with two daughters. What do you mean they have a son? Find me an old woman instead.

Uncle Ernesto's voice sounded like when you slam the door behind you.

- Mariana, I think you fail to see what a chance this is. You can keep the girls with you all the time; you will have everything you need. I honestly don't understand your hesitation.

The cicadas went on buzzing, undisturbed.

A few days later, Ernesto knocked at the door in the dead of night. His pounding woke me up, and when I opened my eyes, I saw that mom was ready to go. She had her good dress on, and she lad lined the bags near the door. I got scared for a moment, but then I saw how neatly she had arranged the clothes for Paloma and me to put on at the other end of our mattress. I shielded Paloma's eyes with my open hand to make sure she doesn't suddenly wake up to think mom's leaving without us.

- Palomita, you have to wake up, I whispered as mom was opening the door for uncle Ernesto.

- We have to get dressed and go.

Paloma rolled to her other side, grunting, so I caressed her hair.

- We're going to a beautiful place.

Uncle Ernesto and mom walked in front of us carrying all the luggage, and I was holding Paloma's hand, walking in their steps. Paloma liked to drag her feet and stir the dust. Mom hadn't made me wear my shoes.

- Since we're leaving, you'll start school when we get there. It's best to keep them safe and new in the bag.

Paloma had stirred so much dust that my eyes began to sting. Looking back, our little hut was no longer visible through the dusty curtain, and I felt tears starting to flow down my cheeks.

Uncle Ernesto threw our luggage in the trailer, and we sat on them. I didn't know the other people in the trailer, which means they had come by truck from somewhere else. Everyone was seated on their luggage.

Ernesto gave some money to the driver.

- Hold on tight; it's going to be a rough ride, the driver said.

When he hugged us goodbye, I had the impression that he, too, had tears in his eyes from all the dust Paloma had stirred.

Not to get bored, half of the way, I drew things with my fingers on Paloma's feet. Her skin is brown, like mine, and as the summer draws to an end, it gets almost black. She was covered in translucent dust that looked white on her skin, a perfect beautiful canvas. I drew birds, turtles, huts, and a river on her right foot, and on her left foot, I drew trees. I covered it all in drawings: from her toes to her knees.

- You're so small, Paloma, I said.

- There's no place left for us.

I looked at mom, but she seemed absent-minded. Her gaze seemed to search for something far away as if she had forgotten that we were there. But she hadn't forgotten; I knew it well. Mom never forgets.

A toothless lady with wrinkled skin started singing. Her voice sounded as if it wasn't hers. It was warm and clear, and it seemed much younger than the woman herself. Although she was singing softly, her song was somehow rising above the sound of the bouncing truck. Paloma had fallen asleep. Her head was in my lap, and some of the men were wiping their eyes with the shirt sleeves.

In her song, a boy had left home and, after walking a long, long way, he could still feel that the air smells of home. He was amazed and thrilled to see that there had been no reason for his fear. The entire world smells like home. The whole world is home. We are home wherever we go. But then he caught a glimpse in his knapsack of the small bread - still warm and still sweet-smelling - that his mom had baked for him early that morning.

When I woke up, the car had stopped in a queue that was slowly advancing towards a green booth. Armed men in uniforms approached the drivers with severe-looking faces, one at a time. Papers were passed back and forth. When we passed the green booth, the truck picked up speed again, and I fell back asleep.

Everyone else got out before us: we were the last ones. Mom asked the driver something through the small window behind him.

- We're entering the city, she said.

All of a sudden, everything looked like nothing I knew, and nothing made sense. Mom's eyes widened, and then she lifted Paloma in her arms and pushed her face against her shoulder. She smiled at me encouragingly, but I knew that she had never seen anything so hideous and absurd, and so many people packed together, so much movement and rattling everywhere. I thought: how fortunate that the old lady with the beautiful voice has already left. Her song would be lost here.

The smell of the city was also strange and disgusting. At home, it smells of grass and dust, sometimes of wet leaves and puddles. Once, our cat Pico hid a dead rat in the house. For a few days, the house smelled terrible, and we couldn't see where it comes from. Mom looked everywhere. She was spending all her time looking. It took some time until she found the rat, almost rotten, hidden near the top of a slipper. This is how the city smells.

The truck brought us in front of a palace. Mom says it's a house, but I think she didn't take a good look. The biggest building I've ever seen before was our school. I haven't been inside, but I heard it has three rooms. This house has a hundred windows and a huge garden in front. The fence in front of it is very tall, and yet above it, you can still see the top floor of the house.

Señora Marta is very beautiful and wears a dress full of frills. She is thin and very, very white, and as soon as we arrive, she acts as if she's known us forever. Señor Antonio is very serious.

- Cuidado, Hector, cuidado, he says once, every two minutes.

Hector is a year older than me. He's wearing shorts with suspenders and has curly golden hair. I've never seen golden hair before. He may be a prince.

Seeing Paloma, señora Marta starts marveling as if at something incredible. She crouches down in front of her, and I can see she barely resists hugging her.

- My, she's so sweet! she exclaims. She is simply adorable!

Paloma has the smallest nose, black curls, and grey eyes surrounded by green rims. Everyone says Paloma looks like an angel. I have known her since she was born, and I can confirm: Paloma is an angel.

Señora Marta put us in a white room, very white, with a big window the wall's size letting in all the afternoon's sunlight. There are bright sheets on the bed. I never knew such white things existed. On the wall above the bed, there is an icon with Saint Mary. Saint Mary has a gentle face and a loving smile. Just like señora Marta.

Señora Marta went away with Mom to show her what she needs to know. As they walked down the hall, I heard her say:

- In a few days, when I'll be less busy, we have to go downtown to buy clothes for the girls.

Half of Hector's face showed through the door opening - I could only see one of his eyes and half of his mouth. He stayed still for a while, weighing things, thinking about how to get started. I waited because he was older and this was, after all, his house.

- Where did you come from? he finally asked when the silence was about to get weird.

I didn't know how to answer that question. At home, we named places after things: down by the river, by the school, at the market.

- Mom says it's from Guatemala. He went on when he saw I didn't answer. Guatemala is as good a name as any other.

Apart from us, there's only Ignacio, señor Antonio's driver. He does the shopping. Señora Marta told mom that Ignacio is very kind-hearted and will help her a lot.

- He used to help Ilaria - God bless her soul - every day. I don't think Ilaria ever went shopping. She just used to make a list and send Ignacio to buy everything she needed. If you want to do the same, you have my blessing.

Mom has been very silent since we arrived. It's not that she doesn't like it here, but she says she doesn't want to disturb. She spends her days cooking and cleaning, working in the garden. Mom is very diligent.

- I am lucky to have you. I am too lucky. Señora Marta says.

- Hector is audacious.

- He missed having kids around, says mom. I think she finds it hard to believe that Hector's first thing in the morning is to come by and bring us cookies. Two days ago, he climbed in one of the trees in the back yard, and he was calling after Paloma and me to follow him up. I told him Paloma's too young to climb trees.

- You climb up alone then.

- I can't just leave her here. She's delicate and gets scared easily, I yelled, tightening my hold of Paloma's hand for her to understand I'm not leaving her.

In fact, I'm afraid to climb trees.

School is only a few days away, and señora Marta laments every day.

- Oh, today again, I don't have time to take the girls shopping. At the latest on Saturday, we have to do it.

Mom says I could go to school dressed in the clothes I already have, but she didn't take a look at the people passing by. Hector pulls my hand and takes me to the front fence. We rest our heads on the cold metal, and we look through the fence posts. The girls walk by wearing colorful skirts with flowers. They all wear light shoes and white socks with ruffles. The women wear hats. Hector pulled my hand and pointed to our left.

- Look, see the lady coming up the street? It's our neighbor from the yellow-and-red house. She has recently given birth. See, there in the perambulator, there's a baby. His name is Matthieu.

There were too many complicated words in what he'd just said. I tried saying Matthieu, Matthieu, but it didn't sound properly. Hector crouched and started laughing, hitting his knees with his palms.

I wonder how they're going to call Matthieu. Paloma's nickname is Palomita, and mine is Mili. It's easy.

Today Hector came to our room grinning from ear to ear. He looked impish as if he had a crazy plan. He didn't speak to us from outside the room like he usually does. He came near the corner where I was playing horse riding with Palomita and whispered to me.

- I want to show you something. Get dressed and follow me.

I gave myself a quick look, and then I checked out Paloma.

- We're already dressed.

- This is all you have?

I didn't quite get what he was asking.

- I have another shirt.

Hector grimaced.

- It's ok, this is fine too. Let's go, we're-going-downtown-to-see-something-phenomenal.

He said this as if he was sharing a top-secret.

- But Paloma doesn't have shoes, I said, and I blushed for no reason at all.

- That's ok, I'll hold her.

We left the yard creeping like ghosts. Hector closed the big gate one millimeter at a time, making sure it wouldn't creak. When it was finally shut behind us, we turned left and started running down the street. It was the first time I was leaving the courtyard. I couldn't help but thinking, what would happen if mom found out.

- You've done this before, going out alone? I asked Hector, panting.

Hector lifted his chin and suddenly became a man.

- I do it almost every day.

I don't think that was true. I hadn't seen him leave the house alone since we've gotten here. I knew almost everything he did because señora Marta left him in mom's care when she had things to do. When he wasn't playing with us, he was supposed to read five pages upstairs, in his room. I don't think he could sneak out of his window.

When we turned the corner, there was suddenly hell. The quiet little street that I used to watch through the fence posts was pouring into a sea of chaos. Small, large, and huge cars were rushing in all directions, honking and retching hot stinking air with a crazed fury. They were fighting for every meter and seemed to escape disaster every second.

I was afraid I would lose Hector. I almost burst into tears, so I clung to his shirt as if for life. I thought: at least he's holding Paloma. They'll get home safe. If I get lost and die, at least she'll be safe.

Hector turned his head and shouted.

- We have to reach the square in the middle, that's where the station is. When you see no more cars passing, run to the other side.

But the cars kept on passing. After each car passing by, Hector looked like he's about to jump through, but I kept pulling him back.

- What are you doing? We need to cross; it's free now.

But I couldn't bring myself to it, as long as there were any cars in sight. In fact, I didn't want to go anywhere anymore.

- I want to go back!

- Don't be silly; there's no reason to be afraid. I'll show you something fabulous.

He pulled me sharply by the hand. I had my eyes closed. I thought: neck or nothing, as long as Paloma is fine.

In the end, we were all fine. We were standing in the square as on an island in the middle of the furious ocean. All around us, the world shrieked with piercing noises. It seemed ready to burst.

- What are we doing here? I asked Hector.

- We're waiting for the tramway, he said casually.

I had no idea what he's talking about. The words Hector uses don't mean anything. I know the names of all the birds that nest on the riverbank. I know the names of the fish and when fruits are ripe. If I hurt my knee, I look for a particular plant, crush it on a boulder, and spread the paste on the wound. But Hector's words don't mean anything.

When the huge thing approached, Paloma started screaming like crazy. Hector's eyes widened.

- Why is she screaming?

- She's never seen a tramway, I replied.

Hector shrugged and passed her on. I held her tight to my chest and tried to calm her down.

- There, there, Paloma, it's just a big car.

Paloma was crying, disconsolate, while Hector counted some coins for a gentleman dressed in a great uniform.

- Where did you find those? he asked, glancing us over.

- They're my cousins from the countryside, Hector replied.

The world is passing by our windows like a hasty animal. My heart beats to break my chest. Hector grins full of himself.

A week ago, I was sitting on the riverbank looking for pebbles. I know a place where the river makes a small swirl, and it sounds lovely. If you are patient, you can see fish jumping in the air. Paloma laughs and claps, delighted. A little down the river, there's a place as quiet as a lake. The water doesn't move at all. It doesn't make a crease. I pull Paloma next to the edge and hold her hand tightly. We look at ourselves in the water. Paloma stares in wonder. She always stares in wonder. She marvels at everything.

Hector says we've got three stations to go. I don't know what stations are, but Paloma's lower lip is curled downwards, and I can hardly wait to get out of here.

Hector says: next station is ours. He pulls me by the hand to the door. A lady with a hat stands behind, examining us.

- What a cute little girl! Is she your sister? she asks Hector.

I may not understand everything, but this lady is dying to know more. She can't truly believe that Paloma is Hector's sister, so she's trying to find out what could possibly bring us together. Hector wears a shirt with cufflinks and a bow tie. Paloma is bare feet and wears an old dress, which I also wore when I was her age. Paloma may have an angel's face, but she cannot look like Hector's sister, so I stick my tongue out to the prying old lady as we get off.

Hector pulls my hand as we squeeze between the hundreds of people blocking our way, clogging everything, standing in each other's path like undisciplined animals. Where do all the people come from? If each of us will become an eagle or a donkey in another life, how come there are so many of us and not so many of them? We used to watch out for the eagles back home to tell us if the forest bursts with animals. Then our neighbors and uncle Ernesto would go hunting. Not my dad. He was almost never home. And when he was, mom told us not to wake him, or we'll be sorry. Better off sleeping than ruining our joy, she used to say.

All of a sudden, Hector stops and turns to us sharply, pointing upwards:

- Ta-daaaa!

I spell the letters, trying to remember what Manuel taught us.

- He-r-n-an-dez. Fa-miii-ly ph-pho-to-grrrraaa-ph-yyy.

I look at Hector, puzzled.

Hector laughs and pulls us inside. There's a bell clinging to the door, and it jingles as we walk through. It's the first beautiful sound I heard ever since we arrived in the city, so I put Paloma down, and I do it again: ding-a-ling!

A spectacled man appears from behind a curtain. I assume he's Hernandez. I can't tell what's Hector has come here for, but I hope we'll be done quickly.

Hernandez examines us as if he's about to buy us. Hector explains to him something I don't quite get, and then he shows him some money. Hernandez looks extremely puzzled, his forehead frowning like an accordion. It looks like he can hardly believe Hector's words. He looks at the money and then at us, loathingly.

- In this state?

Hernandez ended up accepting Hector's money, but he says he cannot take our photographs in this state. Luckily for you, you'll find a basket filled with all kinds of accessories in that corner, he says. He makes us look in the basket to find something appropriate for Paloma and me.

- Appropriate for what? I whisper in Hector's ear.

- For you and Paloma, he repeats confidently.

I don't understand anything, and yet I start searching. I have never seen so many dresses and hats. I found something that looks like a long snake made of feathers. Hector likes it, and he wraps it around his neck.

- See, I look like señora Fernandez, he says, puckering his lips. Little one, be a gentleman, help an old lady climb these stairs!

I feel like laughing, and I don't. I'm afraid mom had a heart attack seeing that we're gone. And I still don't understand what we're doing here.

Hector finally brings himself to explain it to me. He came down here with his father yesterday to have his pho-to-graph taken for the school album. Photographs are being taken with that big black box. It's a bit like looking in a mirror, only that it stays printed on a piece of cardboard.

- Like when we look at ourselves in the river's water, Palomita, I shout triumphantly.

For Paloma, I found a white dress with cream ruffles and laces. It's a little big for her, but if she's seated, you can't tell. Hernandez's eyes grew large as plates when he saw Paloma. He asked her to sit on the big chair in the middle of the room and started turning on lights and looking in the big black box. He said he'd like to photograph Paloma alone first and that her photograph will be his gift to us. Afterward, he'll take a picture of the three of us, since this is why we're here.

- We'll keep it forever as a memory, Hector rejoiced, clapping his hands.

Hector and I stood behind Hernandez and watched what he was doing. I think he took a hundred photographs. He couldn't stop. He keeps telling Paloma to look left, to look right, to lift her chin up, to look serious, to smile, to look dreamy, and all this while he's giggling and mumbling to himself.

- Fabulous! he exclaims every now and then, with one eye looking through the hole, just like Hector and I look at the passing girls through the holes in the house's fence.

Paloma sits quietly on the chair and smiles. She has no idea how beautiful her angel face is amid the jumble of white ruffles and laces. Her curls fall over the massive shoulders of the dress and her round sweet cheeks. Paloma lifts both her plump little hands and pushes the curls off her face using all her fingers. Her eyes shine.

Dressed like this, Paloma looks like a señorita. You wouldn't know that one week ago, I was drawing things for her in the sand using the feathers of a chicken that my mother had slaughtered. One of the feathers had blood on its tip, so I used it to draw a dog's muzzle. But it didn't look good. The blood turned black, mixed with the dust, so I tossed it away, unhappy. But Paloma liked it still, and she started clapping and jumping around the dog.

- Woof woof!

Mom shouts at Paloma, going in with the plucked chicken.

- Little doggy, Paloma, say *doggy*!

Paloma's feet were covered with dust from all the jumping around, so mom brought a cup filled with water and poured it all on her feet. Underneath her, the dust turned into mud.

- Look, you can knead cornbread now, mom said while we were playing in the mud.

Paloma loved to play in the mud and knead cornbread, which she would then feed to her imaginary animals. All her animals eat cornbread, and she gets mud everywhere, even in her hair.

How will Paloma knead cornbread for her animals from now on? She now sits on a very high chair and cannot reach the ground with her feet. Instead of mud, she has two blue ribbons in her hair, and her lovely head is surrounded by loops and ruffles, floating around her like white foam. She's not scared anymore, and she smiles like she's understood that we'll have this memory forever. Dressed like this, she is, and she is not Paloma. She looks as if she's come here in a car with a driver...

she was born in a house with a hundred rooms and many floors...

she's being served breakfast every morning by a woman wearing a dark grey apron over a dress with a white lace collar.

Hector whistles admiringly.

Paloma looks just like a real señorita.

REMEMBERING LEONARD

JACK HALLIDAY

THE WIND WHISTLED THROUGH THE TREES, AND MY LITTLE PUG SHOOK his head to free himself of the stray leaves assaulting his velvety soft ears. He looked up at me with his familiar smile and knowing gaze.

Quickly, he trotted off, up and over the slight nob of a hill, in search of yet another headstone to mark for posterity. How many similar monuments and memorials had likewise been anointed by my little canine confidant in the nearly dozen years he had served as my best friend?

But none like this one.

The engraving caused the particulars to stand out in bold relief before my tired and time-worn eyes.

Leonard Moreland
Beloved Son and Brother
Born 3/19/53 Died 7/4/2014

An entire life reduced to three lines etched in faux marble didn't seem enough. As though time and talents, hurts and hauntings, whims and whispers could be compressed into one final farewell recorded with antiseptic precision by cold and callous machine tooling.

I hugged myself in the chill air, squinted, blinked, and squeezed a tear from each of my eyes as I stood and stared at the only visible remains of a life that had been all too brief and all too sad.

It was one of the most unusual weeks of my young life, the time I spent with my cousins, some forty years ago. I remembered it distinctly because it wasn't too long before my father unexpectedly passed away. It was the week when I met Leonard.

My parents were called away by an extended family emergency, and my aunt Emily and uncle John kindly offered to have me stay with them and their two sons and daughter for the week.

I had never been too close to my cousins since their apartment was some distance from my family, we didn't have a car, and they lived in "the projects."

Even though I was only about ten years old at the time, that phrase communicated that something was "different" about them to my young mind, making them seem even poorer than we were. There was a dim memory of something about my uncle's drinking and my aunt divorcing and then remarrying him, making the same mistake twice, and that after an initial marriage to another man had faltered and failed. I recalled boisterous family gatherings, my uncle's rowdy behavior, and my parents laughing about it on the bus ride home.

These facts engendered a bit of anxiety in me as I contemplated my forced visit. The apprehension didn't abate the morning that my other aunt stopped the car and deposited me in the vast low-income housing development parking lot. The sunlight hurt my eyes, and I squinted as my aunt Emily took the bag from my mother's other sister. They spoke for a few moments about nothing in particular, and then the car drove off, abandoning me to whatever the fates had ordered for my brief stay.

Although I was somewhat afraid and ill at ease in my new surroundings, I was sternly warned by my cousin, Louie, who shared my birthday, but was four years older, that I was to depend on him. I wouldn't get hurt by any of the "tough kids" who lived in the apartment houses adjacent to his. Needless to say, that was all the warning my young and relatively innocent ears needed to hear!

That week was a whirlwind of excitement and experiences I had never encountered in my relatively calm suburban life. It was summertime, and we ran free; and by free, I mean by my cousins' standards, not those of my parents nor any of my friends' families. That "freedom" involved staying up all hours, watching any and all television programs we desired, eating all the candy and drinking all the soft drinks we could comfortably hold, smoking the remains of discarded cigarettes, lighting fires in the garbage dump, and generally causing all kinds of ruckus: the thrill of not getting caught furnishing the fuel for the fire of our adolescent exploits.

But the most unusual episode of the entire week occurred the night before I was to board the bus for home.

It was the evening I was introduced to Leonard.

It was just getting on sunset when Louie exclaimed, "Hey, let's go over to Leonard's apartment!"

"No, he's weird," replied my cousin, Betsy.

"Yeah, I know; that's what makes him so cool! He knows all kinds of weirdos!" Tim, my youngest cousin, started laughing. "Yeah, let's go; Leonard's goofy! Let's go see what he's doin'!" Betsy reluctantly agreed, adding, "But don't make fun of him, okay?" "Why should we?" Louie asked. And we were off.

We crossed yards, ran through alleyways, inched along concrete walls, their rough surfaces clawing at my shirt. After what seemed like an hour (though it could only have been minutes), we finally arrived at our clandestine and mysterious destination.

We all giggled as Louie pounded on the battered door to the apartment. "Leonard? Come on out; we're all here, and we want you to meet our cousin!" His knocking was responded to by absolute silence, the kind that greets you at a funeral home. He looked at us, shrugged, and then repeated the process. I must admit, even with the silence and before I ever laid eyes on Leonard, my spine tingled with something akin to fear and for no logically understandable reason.

A foreboding seemed to spread through me. I wanted to be back home, with Corky, my beagle, in the worst way. But I was doomed now, a prisoner of cousins with whom I wasn't really all that comfortable.

How happy I was that, regardless of what happened tonight, I'd be relatively safe, back in my own home, by morning. I wiped my perspiring forehead with the back of my forearm and realized I felt rather weak and overheated. I would later discover I'd been running a fever of over 100 degrees for several days.

Suddenly, Betsy offered, "Hey, maybe he's over at the old bag's house." Young Tim agreed.

"Doesn't he do something or other to her hair about once a week?" Louie snapped his fingers as he responded. "That's right; why didn't I think of that. Come on."

With that, we were off again, trotting briskly down the metal stairs and out through the heavy metal door, the worn hinges objecting with their low-pitched squeals.

It was almost dark when we entered yet another of the "cookie-cutter" apartment buildings that made up this barracks of buildings built for civilians slowly succumbing to the terminal disease of poverty.

The heavy odor of stale cigarette smoke greeted us as we entered the kitchen of an elderly woman whose nickname, I was informed, was Aunt Grace. She was a spindly little number with small green eyes the color of faded emerald that darted back and forth behind age-old spectacles. Seated in a small, dilapidated kitchen chair at a similarly shabby table all but obscured by ashtrays, newspapers, and half-full coffee cups, a smile worked tiredly at the corners of her wrinkled mouth.

"Hey, Leonard! What's goin' on?"

Louie's loud greeting was answered by a slight nod from the rotund young man towering over Grace. His pudgy fingers were working their cosmetic magic on her gray hair, spinning it into a chorus of curls to be locked in place by one of the many bobby pins in the grip of his chubby, lipsticked lips.

His mumbled response was, "Just fixing her up a bit. She'll be 'ready for her close up, Mr. DeMille' anytime now."

I had no idea what that meant, and it wouldn't have mattered if I did. I was too mystified by the sight of a man in his twenties wearing makeup, Capri pants, and what appeared to be some kind of "wrap-around" blouse. He might as well have been from outer space as far as I was concerned. At that young age, I was completely uninformed about unusual sexual proclivities.

"Who's the little guy?" he asked with a smile.

"He's our cousin, Joey," Betsy replied.

"Hiya, Joey," Leonard said, with what looked like a genuine smile.

For some reason, even at first glance and without any conversation passing between us, I felt a deep sadness for him. He seemed ill-at-ease with himself, and us, for that matter. But when he went back to his work, he seemed to relax as Grace returned to her brand of juicy gossip. She and Leonard giggled, and Louie turned his back to them and put a finger to his lips just before Tim could cut loose with a laugh of his own: at Leonard.

"What's up with him?" I asked on the way back to the apartment.

The three of us stood under the streetlight, Tim tossing large stones from the parking lot at the mound of dirt on the adjacent hillside, gaining additional height with each throw. Betsy sat on the trunk of a parked car, cheering him on. Louie stood in front of me with his hands in his back pockets.

"We're not sure. Seems like his mom died, I think, and he was raised by his dad, who's a real drunk. He told us his father hit him a lot and even came at him with a knife once. I remember one day when he lifted up his sweatshirt and showed us a scar that ran from his waist clean up to his armpit. Poor Leonard."

"Why's he dress like that, with makeup and stuff?" I continued.

"Oh, that. I think somethin' happened to him, you know, some kind o' creepy sex stuff, I think, when he was real young. He says he just feels more comfortable dressing like he does now. Go figure."

Years passed, and I forgot all about that week and my meeting Leonard. Occasionally, he would come to my mind, especially after

I'd gotten old enough to know exactly what he'd become and what had likely happened to him as a little boy. Sometimes I would find myself breathing a prayer for him.

Then, about ten years ago, during a Christmas family gathering, my cousin Louie mentioned him. He said he'd run into him at a dance hall of some type. Leonard was working as a DJ and still dressing the same way. The two of them talked, and Louie got a bit more information from him about his upbringing. It happened that Leonard had discovered his deceased mother had actually been married twice and that his biological father hadn't been the one who had molested him, but his stepfather. He told Louie that knowing that had made him feel a bit better about things in some way he couldn't quite explain. Unfortunately, he had been unable to discover any information about his real father. He assumed he was deceased.

About a month ago, my cousin Louie called requesting information about an investment (I'm a financial consultant).

After we had discussed the particulars of his situation, he suddenly added, "Hey, before I forget, I thought you'd be interested to know that Leonard died. You remember Leonard?"

Somewhat stunned, I found myself mumbling, "Yeah, Leonard; sure, I remember him. What happened?"

"Finished up with AIDS, alone in a local hospital."

"No, kidding," I replied mechanically.

"Sad, ain't it?" Louie added.

"It is; hey, what was his last name again?" I asked.

After I hung up, I began the computer search that finally filled in the rest of the blanks regarding Leonard's background. That information was what brought me here, today, on this bleak and dreary fall afternoon.

My pug temporarily broke my reverie as he trotted down the hill toward me. He stopped dead at my feet and then stood at attention. A little canine sentry guarding me in my grief, his large kind eyes fixed on the marker that was even now receiving my teardrops as an inarticulate goodbye to the remains of a once innocent life, wrecked and ruined by the selfish lust of a stepfather.

I sighed and decided to linger just a few minutes more, remembering Leonard.

My brother.

MONTANA POW WOW

RICHARD LEIST

LYMAN FERRIS AND PEPPER REDFIELD SIPPED LONGNECK PACK TRAIN beer, boots off, stretched out on folding lawn chairs in the cargo bed of Pepper's '87 Chevy pick-up. They watched shadows lengthen over the Bear Paw Mountains 10 miles to the south of Havre, Montana, parked in their usual spot near the old timber bridge. Lyman pulled another beer from the Yeti cooler between them and twisted off the cap. It was early May. Swallows circled and soared in a cloudless sky. A pale sliver of moon appeared over the treetops to the east.

"Nice night," Pepper said. "Time you got?"

Lyman pulled a cell phone from the front pocket of his flannel jacket.

"8:07."

Pepper nodded.

"We got time to drink two more beers."

"Three," said Lyman. "Get going. I'm a half beer ahead of you."

"You know your feet stink," Pepper said. "Put your boots back on."

Lyman inhaled.

"Do not. It's your truck bed. Hauling garbage again?"

Pepper tapped a cigarette halfway out of a pack and offered it to Lyman. Then he tapped one out for himself, patting his pockets for a lighter. Lyman clanked open a Zippo and held it up for Pepper to lean in and get a light. Their faces glowed in the flame. Lyman lit his, took a deep drag, and blew smoke rings into the stillness.

"You tell Grace, where you were headed?"

Pepper nodded.

"She knows."

"She know you were going to be with me?"

Pepper nodded again.

"She care?" Lyman asked.

"Maybe."

"She talk to you about it?"

"Little."

"She have an opinion?"

Pepper leaned back and chugged his beer, taking a moment to let out a loud burp. He leaned over and grabbed another from the cooler. "Let me catch up. Train's coming at 8:23."

"Always does," Lyman said. He looked at his cell phone.

"We got 10 minutes."

He chugged his beer, sucked on his cigarette, and reached for another beer.

"Drink up. We gotta have good ammo."

Pepper twisted off the bottle cap on the new beer.

"To answer your question, she cares."

"About me?" Lyman asked.

Pepper winced and shook his head no.

"Not you. Mandy. You know they still talk."

Lyman took a slug of his beer and didn't speak right away.

"She cheated on me.

Think Gracie knows that?"

Pepper stood up and looked down at his buddy.

"Hell, are you kidding? I didn't know that! Doubt Gracie did. When did this happen?"

"A couple months back when we were working overtime putting up the water tower."

Pepper chugged his beer.

"What time you got?"

"8:17."

"How many beers we had?"

Lyman stood up.

"Thinking seven apiece." He flicked his cigarette off the back of the pick-up into the dirt.

Pepper watched.

"Shitty distance, man. Watch this." He flicked his off the back, arcing the glow into the shadows.

"Chug that beer," Lyman said. "We gotta move."

Pepper leaned way back, drained his in three gulps, and jumped off the back of the truck.

"Race you to the top."

Lyman laughed.

"I'm walking. My bladder is freakin full."

They trudged together up the dirt-covered planks of the heavy timber bridge built in 1957 by the farmers' co-op to haul tractors, combines, and supplies to distant fields. It smelled of creosote, especially when there was no breeze.

"Man, I gotta piss," Pepper said.

"Come on, Amtrak. Come on, Empire Builder," Lyman mumbled.

"Hope this one has one of them big dome scenic cars! What do they call it?"

"You're talking the 'View Liner.' How about three of them bad boys?"

"Ever piss on the on-coming side?" Pepper asked.

"Kidding? It'd blow up in your face."

They edged to the west side and listened for the train.

Lyman sang in a low, gravelly voice, "I hear the train a-coming, it's coming round the bend, And I ain't see the sunshine since I don't know when..."

"Five dollars says I can pee from the first locomotive all the way to the end of the train," Pepper said as he unbuckled his heavy leather belt and dropped his pants.

"Here, she comes! I'll take that bet!" Lyman yelled. He grabbed the shiny pistol-shaped belt buckle on his blue jeans and dropped his pants to his ankles.

Their pale white buttocks glowed like back-lit birthday balloons.

Beneath their feet, the bridge began to vibrate. Then it shook. The parallel tracks suddenly shined like polished iron in the intensity of the Empire Builder headlight. Seventeen passenger cars and two locomotives passed below them like silver bullets at 65 miles an hour. Both boys arched their backs and started pissing, letting loose with barbaric yawps in the roar of the train. They could see the blur of the passengers in the scenic cars, knowing none would be aware of the two high school graduates from Havre, Montana, expressing their opinions with golden streams of urine.

In twenty-five seconds, the train was nearly out of sight. They watched as the last train lights faded westward. Tree frogs began to chirp. Galaxies of stars, constellations were suddenly visible in the night sky. It was as quiet as a church sanctuary.

"I won," Lyman whispered.

"Hell, you did," Pepper said, "and why are you whispering?"

"I'm still dripping, and you ain't." Lyman started laughing. "You owe me five

bucks."

"No way I do," Pepper said, grunting to no avail in an effort to pee just a little more. Lyman bent over, grabbed his underpants and drawers, and stood up. He looked at Pepper and said, "You lose. And pull up your pants, you big dummy."

They walked off the bridge and re-took their positions in the back of the pick-up.

"So Gracie didn't know Mandy cheated?" Lyman asked.

Pepper reached into the cooler and grabbed two long necks with his big hand.

"Your name's on this one," he said, offering the beer to Lyman.

He took it, twisted off the cap, and took a big gulp, wiping his jacket sleeve across his face. "You'll tell Gracie for me?"

Pepper nodded. It was quiet for a minute. They could hear the breeze begin to pick up in the trees. Finally, he broke the silence.

"It usually helps me to piss on the train. Tonight not so much. Did it help you?"

Lyman took another swig and nodded thoughtfully.

"It helps to get the truth out. Be good if your wife and family still like me."

"You know the Indians around here share a pipe when they discuss their problems," Pepper said. He tapped out a cigarette and handed it to Lyman.

"Well, we ain't Indians, but they're onto something. For us, it's pissing on the Empire Builder."

"Think it does us any good?" Pepper asked.

Lyman nodded.

"Doesn't hurt."

THE FROZEN LAKE

AUSTIN MANCHESTER

I STEPPED TO THE LAKE, MY FEET ALMOST TOUCHING THE FROZEN SHEET of ice. Just a few months ago, my brother and I stood on this very spot about to push our little boat out onto the water. We were on a quest to fish and to catch and release turtles.

Calvin stopped loading our fishing gear into the boat. "Ya know," he started, "when you see me next, I'll be looking a lot different." He ran his hand through his tousled hair and let out a laugh. "Can't have this where I'm going. Also gonna be a lot bigger." He looked down both of his arms and squeezed real tight, trying to show off whatever muscles he thought were there.

"Why will you be so different?" I stared at my brother, trying to memorize his boyish features. His long, curly brown hair, his sharp nose, dented from when he broke it during a four-wheeler accident a few summers ago. Mom wasn't too happy about that. She cussed him out real good, saying he should've been smarter, shouldn't have been riding without a helmet in the woods. Calvin was never really one for helmets.

"Well, the army makes you tough, kiddo. Guys bulk up and get tattoos and fire guns and become men."

Calvin needed some bulk.

I sat in the boat, and he handed me the fishing poles. He pushed the boat into the water and hopped in. We churned our feet around and around to move to the center of the lake. We stopped and floated and cast our lines out.

"Calvin?"

"Yeah, Barry?"

"Are you going to kill people?"

"Whoa, Barry. Well, I mean… I might have to. Yeah. It's gonna be my job to protect you, protect mom, protect this country. There's a lot of bad people out there, Barry."

"That's scary," I whispered.

"Oh, hey!" Calvin pulled up on his line. "I think I got one!" He fought, roping his line in, and pulled out a tiny fish, not even bigger than my hand. "Look at this little guy." He took the fish off the hook. "Back ya go!" Calvin yelled and tossed the fish into the water.

"I still don't get why you have to go."

"You're too young to understand—"

"I'm ten! I'm old!"

"Okay, bud, sure, sure. But, Barry, there's just nothing left for me out here."

"There's me and mom."

"Right, right, there's you guys." He put his arm around me and squeezed my shoulder. "But my future, little bud—it's somewhere else. Somewhere out in the world. Somewhere where I gotta go and find it. You'll understand when you're older. You're smart, Barry. When you're my age, you'll figure out that the only way for you to become something is to leave these woods."

He relaxed his arm and looked out over the lake, the expression on his face one I did not understand.

I started to lose feeling in my feet. I could barely notice the cold snot resting on my upper lip. I dug my hands deep into my pockets, trying to keep them warm. I released my breath, watched it disperse in the cold winter air.

The suit my mother had put me in wasn't comfortable or warm. I felt out of place in it. Everyone had said, "Barry, you look so grown up," or, "Barry, you're such a handsome little man." An aunt had told me, "You're the man of the house now, Barry." I hadn't known what to say to that, but I cried with her as she spoke.

"Hey, Barry," Calvin said as we finished packing our gear. He caught two fish and a few turtles, releasing them all. I caught nothing.

The setting sun painted the sky a rich purple. "I want to give you something before I go. And before I forget."

My back was to him, and I didn't want to turn around. I wanted to stay on the lake, stay with the sunset. I wanted to catch a turtle and bring it home.

I picked up a stone and tried skipping it like I had seen him do countless times before, but the stone just plopped into the water and sunk.

"Here." Calvin stuck his hand in front of my face. He held an NBA trading card, a rookie Kevin Garnett—my favorite player. "For you."

I took it and held it firmly in both hands. Another time, from when before Calvin decided to go, I would have ecstatic. I had wanted this card for long.

"But this is from your collection?"

"It's your collection now, Barry." He mussed up my hair and walked away. He grabbed the fishing poles and our cooler and started for back home. I stole another look at the sunset and trotted to catch up with him.

"That card might be worth a pretty penny someday. When I get back, I'll take you to a game. Promise."

The sky was turning black, the stars like pinpricks letting light through a curtain. I fumbled with my tie, trying to loosen it with my hands that were a translucent white, my blue veins visible in the moonlight.

For days now, I had been trying to grasp what had happened. "Barry, your brother's not coming back," Mom said. I had just gotten home from school to find her at the kitchen window. Her hands were limp in the sink amongst the soapy water and dirty dishes. Her eye makeup was running down, her shoulders and legs shaking.

"He won't ever be coming home," she said and then collapsed to her knees, heavy sobs forcing their way out of her.

"Mom, you're scaring me." I hugged myself and shivered, cold even though our heater was running full blast.

I stepped towards her, unsure of what to do. I was the one who cried, and it was her job to make me feel better. I didn't know how to do her job.

"He's gone, Barry. He's gone!" Her shout rang through the house, rattling the walls.

"Calvin? Gone?"

"Oh, Barry." Mom crawled towards me and placed her hands on my shoulders. "Your brother was killed, Barry." More tears fell from her eyes and landed in her open mouth like raindrops on a cloudy day.

She collapsed further still, leaned back against the cabinets. "It's my fault. I should never have let him go. But he was just so stubborn. He insisted that he was a man that he needed to do his patriotic duty. He was a kid. He was a kid!" Mom put her face in her hands and sat still, sat silent.

My body moved on its own, my mind floating somewhere else. I let my backpack and coat tumble down the stairs as I went to our bedrooms. Instead of going to my room, I slowly pushed open the door to Calvin's. His walls were lined with posters of Timberwolves and Twins. On his dresser stood trophies for baseball, football, basketball. On a shelf above his desk, he had displayed a basketball signed by Kevin Garnett.

His bed was neatly made, untouched for too many seasons.

I grabbed the basketball and stood before his bed. I firmly placed my hand on his blanket, disturbing the stillness of his absence. I gripped it tight and then let go. I crawled onto his bed, laying my head upon his pillow. I brought the ball to my chest and tucked my knees under it. I fell asleep thinking about the game that Calvin would never take me to.

"You should go back inside, little bud."

I turned around, astonished to hear his voice. I ran, my feet snapping fallen twigs in two, and jumped into his arms.

"It's real cold out here, and I bet Mom's getting worried about you."

His words didn't matter. I pushed my face further into his chest and his rumpled clothes. He was wearing a suit just like mine: a black jacket and a white shirt. His hair was buzzed down real short. Gone was the tangled mess of curls.

"Come on. I got you." Calvin carried me forward through the dark, dark woods with his now-large arms. I could feel the strength in them underneath his jacket. I rested my head on his muscular shoulder.

"Why did you leave?" I whispered.

"I had a duty to do. I told ya that."

But his answer wasn't good enough.

"Mom says it was her fault."

"It's no one's fault, Barry, except for the damn IED that blew me to bits." He winced. "I'm sorry—you didn't need to hear that."

"You said you'd take me to a game. I was going to wear my KG jersey."

"Oh, gosh, Barry. I know. But..." He looked around for words that weren't there.

"Just...don't do what I did, Barry. Go to school; get a job. Take care of mom. Don't go die in a desert."

I looked at him, trying to figure out if regret or shame was painted on his face. Maybe both.

He set me down as we neared the treeline. Looking into my eyes, he said, "I gotta go now, buddy." He embraced me in the tightest hug he'd ever given. "Bye, Barry." He let go and took a step back.

I wiped my eyes, and when I pulled my hands away, he was nowhere to be found. "Calvin?" I called out for him, but the woods gave no reply.

I turned and entered our house. Mom came running from the living room and threw her arms around me. "Barry! I was getting so worried about you. Where were you?"

"I was at the lake, Mom."

She took her sweater off and draped it on my shoulders. She rubbed her hands along my arms, trying to warm me. "Oh, honey, you're so cold! Why did you go and do that? At this time of night!"

"I wanted to see Calvin."

"Oh, honey..." She frowned. "Come, let's get you to bed. Get you under your blankets and warm you right up." She stood and took my hand, leading me to the stairs. "Everyone left already. They left a lot of food. Too much for just us."

She continued talking, but I stopped listening. Going up the stairs, I turned my head to catch a glance outside the kitchen window. For a moment, I thought I saw a light peering through the trees.

BUTTERFLIES

DON MCLELLAN

After the fighting had stopped, when the worst of the enemies had been expelled from the motherland, and some semblance of calm had been restored, the scribe decides to end his years of wandering and settle in the family's ancestral village. Though he'd left Shin Yang as an infant, and had no living relatives in the area, he remembers what his father had said of its tidal lagoon, that in the heat of the afternoon, "the butterflies, there, consort like sweethearts."

He reached an agreement with the appropriate bureaucrats as to a "service" fee, which includes storage space for his things. He leaves his lodgings every morning for the short walk along the still-impaired village thoroughfare, past the shuttered shops and up the steep, granite steps of the administrative building. Sheets of writing paper held in place by river stones are soon stacked neatly on a foldout table, sharpened pencils and ballpoint pens squeezed into an empty spice jar. He's had the typewriter refurbished, the same clacking machine his father had used. On a busy workday, it's gripped like a cello between his arthritic knees.

He watches from the building's portico as a long line of newcomers and returning residents arrive, possessions stacked in rickety carts or strapped to the weary hides of mules and oxen, angry tails swatting the flies swarming their dung-caked behinds.

Throughout the day, a caravan of rumbling lorries and buses deliver more hopefuls. They stagger bleary-eyed and bewildered through the bustling streets, the air rank with petrol fumes and open sewers.

Business is slow for the first few weeks, but he remains optimistic. After years of upheaval and despair, the new government demands documentation for business transactions, for identification papers, letters of introduction, rental agreements – modernization, it's being called. His landlady, the widow Wu, trapping him in the hallway before he can slip away, says, "More than half the village was destroyed by the shelling. The looters whooped and hollered through the night." An unraveling braid twines along the old woman's twisted spine. Her mouth is filled with rotting stubs.

She waits for him every morning, the man she refers to by his room number, 305. There's an urgency to her utterances, as though she's dictating a last will and testament. "It's a disgrace how long it's taking to rebuild. A lot of the kids don't bother attending school. They'd rather play in the rubble." She sometimes invites him to breakfast in the inn's claustrophobic kitchen. A sweet bean bun purchased fresh from a street vendor, and a steaming cup of cha—a flea-ravaged housecat coils in her lap.

Most of the other residents are single men like him; they keep to themselves, their secrets vaulted. His room is on the top floor, under a water-stained ceiling. The floorboards groan, he can smell mold, yet the monthly charge is affordable, and there are a bathhouse and water closet out back. Each room has a cot, two threadbare woolen blankets, a small desk, and a chair. The inn is connected to an unreliable electrical grid, the reason for the paraffin lamp. He plugs cracks in the walls with rags, but nothing stops the mice. In the morning, he finds their droppings amassed in the northwest corner.

The lone window's view consists of a grey sky hanging like woodsmoke above a rocky onion field and a cypress copse. During typhoons, he can hear waves pounding the shore. "Listen closely, 305," says the widow, her buttonhole eyes impeded by drooping brows, "and you can hear the remains of unlucky fish boats scraping the ocean floor."

He rises before dawn and sits smoking at the open window, from where he sometimes glimpses a man of similar age emerge from the woods just about the time a rooster from a neighboring property begins its hollering. The man appears to be a farmer, with the burnished skin and stooped shoulders of those who work the fields. He stops before the trunk of a magnolia tree; its bark discolored, the branches brittle. "Every spring, it had white blossoms the size of snowflakes," the widow had said, her thoughts trapped in gentler times. "My grandmother made medicine from the leaves. She believed there was no ailment they couldn't cure."

The farmer presses his palms together and bows three times. He then unties the draw securing his trousers, aiming his mustard dribble at the roots pushing up through the ground like some subterranean beast. Emptied, his bare ass as white as fresh linen, he shakes his hose vigorously, as elderly men must, hoists and knots his trousers, and then bows three times again before continuing on his way. Despite the irrigation, the tree continues to wilt. Limbs snap in a breeze. Birds avoid it.

Business picks up. As customers present themselves in the administration building's portico, he attempts to surmise their place in the world by attire, gait, dialect. Does a man puff out his chest, add growl to his voice? Does a woman bat an artificial lash? Does she fuss needlessly with her hair?

All sorts seek his service: those like himself, whose formal schooling had been abandoned due to the strife and the poor, of course, and the indolent. Most customers are farm laborers, domestics, factory hands, folks who'd given up trying to clean their fingernails – comrades, as they've been renamed, for whom plow and scythe and a strong back are essentials, but pencil and paper?

As part of the national reckoning, citizens need the new forms explained, archaic legal terms interpreted. There are wordy registrations for vehicles, fishing vessels, farm animals, property of any kind, all grist for a scribe, an ancient and noble occupation blighted by unstable remuneration. Building permits have to be filled out in duplicate, one copy to the surly clerk. Even after the revolution, every transaction requires a government stamp, and every government stamp requires a discreet monetary incentive.

Contrary to propaganda, the economy is in freefall, and many of his customers have no yuan. In exchange for his assistance, they offer vegetables, tobacco, herbal elixirs, small amounts of opium wrapped in wax paper. Some detect in him a softness of the heart and are quick to exploit it. One such character tries persuading him to "authenticate" that the hundreds of bottle caps he'd stomped flat are coins from an ancient dynasty.

"Make some kind of certificate," he says. "We'll split the proceeds." He declines. The coins during that era were square. They were made of copper. A hole was punched in the middle.

A young musician offers to play his reed flute alongside the scribe's work station in exchange for him appealing an unfavorable land ruling against the family. The scribe grovels to the appropriate official, gifts him a cluster of grapes, a packet of American Sweet Caporal cigarettes, and the decision is overturned. The musical performance is pleasing. It attracts a sizable crowd.

One soggy morning a fisher leaves his bicycle at the foot of the stairs. The man smells of the tides; brine slops inside his hip-waders. "I need my fishing license renewed," he says. "When I'm at sea, the bike is yours." The scribe strokes his chin, counter-offering: his services for the bicycle. "If I'm out of town," he says, "the bike is yours." The fisher yields.

A handsome woman of generous curves – a former showgirl, tattles the widow – claims her incarcerated husband has been unfairly accused of a transgression she notably does not identify. "You'll have to present a convincing letter to dissuade the authorities," he urges. "Sound evidence." She leads him into a corner and bears a small but exquisite breast crowned with an enormous, dark nipple. "How's this for sound evidence?" she says. "Write a good letter. I'll let you shave my bush."

When business slows, and if his knees are up to it, he cycles to the shore. Like his father, he enjoys chasing butterflies in the lagoon. He consults a reference guide to verify the species – most recently, a jezebel, the majestic Delias pasithoe, with its oval spots on a shimmering, ink-black forewing and a yellow dorsal patch. The liberated insect – for whom the average lifespan is just one month – flits from his net, alights atop a morning glory, feasting on the creamy nectar.

He's about to take a break, enjoy a stroll through the village when the brothel owner Hua Ling, who he knows by reputation, stands before him. Two bodyguards shod in heavy military boots patrol the street. After the war, the scribe, who'd fought with the partisans, was able to return to his former occupation, but others were not so fortunate. Some turned to banditry, and some, like this pair, to thuggery.

"A moment of your time," says Hua Ling.

They move to a tea shop in the market. Her protectors monitor the entrance, scanning the passing faces for enemies. The younger of the two, an intense, fidgety sort, has swollen knuckles. The big one has an eye and part of an ear missing. A hasty battlefield repair, he suspects.

Hua Ling skips customary pleasantries. "One of my girls has run off with a piano player. Her friends say he made promises, but what fool will give up his children for a whore? She's tried killing herself several times."

She walks like a man, dresses like a man, and speaks with the directness and forcefulness of one. But despite these efforts to disguise her gender, Hua Ling remains what the creator had intended: a strikingly beautiful creature. Though middle-aged and stout, her complexion is flawless, the lips full. Her monolid eyes reveal nothing. He imagines the face sitting across from him, filling a page in a magazine. Or on a billboard selling liqueur, hair products, a handy new kitchen appliance – anything.

He's to write a letter, she instructs, success to be judged by its ability to persuade the girl to return – to Hua Ling's bed, presumably. He pretends to wrestle with the offer, but he has little choice. He'd accepted too many swaps and is in danger of not making his rent. It's monied customers like Hua Ling who allow him to receive the trades of those who aren't.

"I'm not often asked to author a love letter."

From a leather billfold, she slaps down more yuan than he makes in a month.

"The same amount again if I like it. A bonus if she comes back."

He begins work on the composition that same evening, sketching an outline in the light of the paraffin lamp. At sunrise, the floor strewn with crumpled drafts, he rises stiffly from his chair. His knees ache, his thoughts are sluggish. He hears the rooster crow and glances out the window just as the farmer airs his scrawny backside.

His father taught him the trade, a dissident mandarin sentenced to exile. The family was peripatetic. His father reduced to itinerant work as a scribe. The boy served as his assistant, delivering messages, copying documents, filing paperwork. His mother and younger sister sold purloined vegetables in the street.

As the family could not afford school fees, he hungrily took to the apprenticeship, devouring abandoned books and periodicals. He studied menus, leaflets, street signs, political posters, the labels of care packages from the other side of the world. He poured over discarded newspapers and learned some English from an offshore radio program transmitted by Christians. By the time he was a teen, he could reproduce hundreds of characters from the national script.

His mother, unable to abide the hardships, passed in her sleep one summer night. Some months later, men came for his father, blades flashing, breaths foul with soju. He was found days later swinging like laundry in the sun. An international aid organization arranged an adoption in Canada for his sister. Her name is Chun Tao; it means spring peach. He cannot bite into one without summoning her distraught face.

To honor the memory of those he mourns, the scribe visits a temple every year. He burns incense, makes a modest offering. The observance is also for his wife Shan, who, with most doctors at the front, perished in childbirth, and for their unnamed infant, a girl who'd survived only a few hours.

The door to the past has been breached now, there in his drafty room at the inn, where the mice shit in the corner, and the half-mad landlady hovers in the stairwell spying on her transient residents. He'd slipped the swaddled newborn inside his coat that day and fled into the forest, running until his lungs sputtered. At a bend in the river, he dug a grave in a patch of soft afternoon light.

The Brothel, A hotel in more prosperous times, is outside the village, at the end of a rutted road in the foothills' cool. He pedals the bicycle, his knees throb. He catches his first sight of the property just as night falls, the four stories of the main building and the cottages scattered throughout artfully landscaped grounds. At the main entrance, someone steps from the shadows. "This way." Lamplight spilling through a window identifies him as the disfigured guard.

He's led around the back, up a narrow flight of stairs, along a musty hallway, and into a room smelling of burning briquettes that glow and hiss in a stone fireplace. Hua Ling reclines on a mahogany-framed bed. She wears silk pajamas.

He hands her the letter.

"Read it to me," she says.

He stands before her like an anxious schoolboy. "My dearest Dongmei," he begins. "My heart shattered like glass the day you left my side . . ." It continued like that for two pages, every cliché he could muster, as he knows originality is rarely rewarded. He'd sprinkled the letter with contrition and sentimentality, with bits of lyric from operas, signing off with "Your loving and devoted Hua Ling."

She climbs out of bed and hands him an envelope. He can feel the weight of an encouraging volume of paper currency.

"Nice work," she says. "Let's sit."

She opens a bottle of Scotch, pours two shots; they clink glasses. Assuming their business concluded, he prepares to leave, but she protests. "I don't like drinking alone."

She speaks plainly. "I found Dongmei in a bar up north. We've lived together for a couple of years. She collected debts and managed the girls. Then someone told me they saw her in town with a musician who'd performed here. I know she likes men, too, so I confronted her, but she denied it."

Hua Ling refills her glass and tops off his.

"I discovered she'd been stealing from me and called her on it. She drank some poison, but one of our customers that night was a doctor. She ran off as soon as she was able. We have contacts who say they can get a letter to her."

Her face is flushed, the words slurred; she rambles. She recounts the beatings endured as a child for being different, the indignities when enemy soldiers occupied her village – all of it, he supposes, to justify the indignities she has since foisted on others.

He bathes and slips into clean trousers, and a pressed changshan. The widow corners him about the rent as he's heading out the door. "This is your last warning, 305." A mud-splattered lorrie brakes noisily at the inn's entrance. The younger guard is driving; One Eye is sprawled across the passenger seat. The scribe attempts to engage the latter in conversation, but the brute responds with shrugs, grunts, curses. His butterflies said more.

He's led again to Hua Ling's chambers. She waves him into the chair.

"Dongmei has come home," she says, allowing a rare smile. "I wanted to thank you properly."

An attractive woman he hadn't seen previously enters and confers quietly with Hua Ling, who excuses herself. The woman seems different from the girls he sees leading their customers to the cottages, and it's not that she's older and fully clothed. There's a poise to her, an economy of movement. She sits at the edge of her chair, ankles crossed, shoulders squared, as if posing for a formal photograph.

"Hua Ling asks that you accept her appreciation."

She leads him downstairs and hands him off to a hostess, who leaves him in a dark den subdivided by curtains into private enclaves.

It had been many years since he'd visited such a place. He yearns for his shabby refuge and his notebook of butterfly sightings, the delicious quiet behind a locked door, but three girls block an escape. They are excessively painted, revealingly robed. Their perfumes cause his eyes to water.

"Compliments of Hua Ling," says the tallest. "You can have one, two, or all three of us." The girls cover their mouths and giggle.

"What about the lady that brought me here?"

"Dongmei?" More giggling. "She belongs to Hua Ling."

He wakes early the next morning wanting to spew, his mind still muddled from the dreamy narcotic. He notices his clothes in a heap on the floor and the naked comfort girl asleep on either side of him. The third, between his legs, is also asleep. He carefully removes himself from her mouth.

He leaves the bicycle at the lagoon entrance and traipses around to a mossy clearing on the far bank. The humid air is abuzz with dragonflies, mosquitoes, and honeybees, with the shrill mating call of the cicada and butterflies of every kind and color. Farther back and high up in the trees, a parrot nags incessantly; a magpie trills a mocking reply. It's his favorite place, this, crouched amongst the pineapple lilies, the air scented with jasmine and cinnamon. It's midday, and he has the lagoon all to himself. He was hoping to run down a swallowtail, but the wily insect eludes capture.

He notices her as he's wheeling for home across the flats. In a bright summer dress, squinting into the glare, wrestling the wind for possession of a floppy sunhat. Out on the point, squealing children explore the tide pools. A scattering of pale-skinned bathers is spread out along the shoreline.

"Dongmei, isn't it?"

She fixes a clip to her hair, swats a sandfly.

"The letter writer, yes? You haven't been around.

"I'm still recuperating."

She pats a spot beside her on the blanket, offers him a wedge of her orange.

"You write a nice letter," she says.

"I was nicely reimbursed."

She becomes conscious of the bruises on her arms and shoulders and attempts to conceal them.

"A fall?" he asks, but she grows quiet, lowers her eyes.

"Why did you return? I doubt it was my letter."

"I was told they'd abducted my aunt, who I was close to when I was young, but it was a lie. I learned that several years ago, she'd stepped on an explosive while seeding a rice field."

"She told me you've had difficulties."

"I had a fling with a piano player, it's true. When I tried to break it off, he threatened to tell Hua Ling unless I gave him money. Every time I made a payment, he wanted more."

"She believes her feelings for you are mutual."

"I've had to lie to survive since I was a child. Hua Ling drinks too much. She can be nasty. She also sleeps with some of the others. I've wanted to leave for a long time."

She slides the sundress up her thigh, extends her arms, slips off a shoulder strap. Some of the bruises are old. Others are not.

"The girls are rented out to pay her gambling debts. She's the biggest moneylender in the district, did you know that? All the opium goes through her."

"The country is changing. There could be a place for you."

"Her heavies don't let me out of their sight."

She draws an arrow in the sand. He glances over his shoulder. Poking out from beneath a beach umbrella are two pairs of boots.

Just as some butterflies sense a storm several hours before its arrival, he'd anticipated Hua Ling's appearance at his table. The younger ruffian leans against a wall, nibbling his fingernails. One Eye glares up at him from the bottom step. The front of his smock is stippled with blood.

"I get the feeling the big one doesn't care for me."

"You're wrong," she says, breathing hard from the climb. "Neither of them do."

"How can I help you, Hua Ling?"

"I understand you ran into Dongmei at the beach. I've been told she's planning to run off again. Did she mention it to you?"

"Why would she?"

"Let me know if you hear anything." She grabs hold of the railing but then stops, turns. "I was told you catch butterflies."

"I do."

"Why?"

"So that I can set them free."

Darkness presses in on him, a shiver ripples through his shoulders and down his back. He hears someone coming up the trail, a purposeful stride. He puts a match to the lantern.

"I was afraid you wouldn't come," she says.

"So was I, yet here we are."

"Some of the girls are covering for me, but I couldn't bring my things without raising suspicion."

He hands her a daypack. It contains food and water, a cotton shift and sandals, some cash. He retrieves his bicycle from the bushes.

"If a tire goes flat, dump it in the woods."

"I was hoping you'd join me."

"If I was a younger man, you wouldn't have to ask."

He holds the map up to the light. Runs his finger along the route. "Stay off the main roads. The train stops at Bin Shin."

She leans in and kisses him on the lips, the soft kiss of a lover, then hops on the bicycle and pushes off. She doesn't look back – a good sign. When it had been his time to run, he hadn't either.

Candles Blaze AT the entrance of every home and shanty in Shin Yang; feral dogs fight over the edible offerings left outside the gates. It is the final hour of the final day of the Festival of Hungry Ghosts when the souls of the deceased are said to appear before the living. Incense spices the air, embers spit from the flames of fires set at the crossroads. A sea breeze has made its way into the village, chilling the air.

He detours around a mound of freshly fallen shit.

Though the godless authorities discourage participation in the ancient observance, empty chairs are bunched around dinner tables piled high with seasonal favorites in anticipation of ancestral guests. At the temple, villagers – he, the scribe, amongst them – look on as parchment paper is unfurled and profound words are mumbled. Tears well, monks chant, children, tremble.

He waits afterward at his open window for morning to steal over the land, for the farmer to trundle up to the dying magnolia and the mist to lift from the onion field, but then he hears the old woman cry out from somewhere down below. Tenants on his floor turn their locks, the hallway goes dark. Heavy boots climb the stairs.

PETRA WITH PUNK BAND

SAMANTHA PILECKI

Loud music filled the room, making it hard to hear anything else.

"They're good, right?" Erin yelled.

"They're good," Petra acquiesced. Honestly, she didn't care, and honestly, she didn't know why she'd agreed to see them play. It was something to do. Maybe something would happen.

But she knew, no matter what, she'd remain stone. Unbroken.

"They're here," Erin squealed when she checked her phone. She and Petra went outside, to the band's minivan. The seats had been removed for the equipment. Amps, pedals, cymbals and stands were arranged alongside a Tetris of limbs, sitting unbelted on the floor.

Petra joined them, unafraid. Her skin shone enameled in the reflection of the darkened window. Nothing could chip her. She felt her collar bone's ridged sculpture. Still there, same, solid as rock.

"We need donuts!" announced a blond boy on the floor, in between an amp and a bass drum. He had a long, leonine body and a cherubic mane. Well-muscled. Petra glanced at Erin, raised an eyebrow.

"That's Kevin," Erin confided, seeing her interest. "He's leaving in September for the army."

Petra zeroed in on him then. Whatever was between them, it

already meant nothing. All the boys before had left her intact, and this one would be no exception.

Coffee was obtained and promptly spilled in the parking lot. The multi-purposed cups were refilled with vodka, the donuts consumed.

"*Drunkin* Donuts," the boy Kevin snickered happily as he poured into Petra's cup again. She licked her rough lips, lichen-kissed by powdered donut crumbs.

Same, same, same. But the ride passed quickly. They appeared in the city outside a parking garage, identically gum-stained and piss-reeking as any back home.

Erin looked at the painted symbols on the wall.

"Green C One, Green C One," someone repeated the deck level, a mantra to the religion of memory. Soon the whole band was caterwauling. "Green C Ooooone!" A happy chorus and Petra herself, one silent statue.

"We'll be damned trying to remember this at three a.m.," Erin laughed, and Petra approved with a carved smile. Three a.m. was the proper witching hour, after all. Maybe something would happen then.

The band's equipment-carrying parade caroused on. Petra was entrusted with holding Kevin's guitar.

"Do you like the city?" he asked.

"It's okay," she said, speaking truth. She didn't like or dislike the city. It existed, just like herself.

The city, the sky, the freaks, and smells; they were all there, dependable. Trash bursting from the bags on the curb. Faux sunglasses and designer bags spilling from cheap stands, pretzels slimed with mustard, the homeless squelching into corners with cardboard signs.

The same. Petra fit in with the lions at the library, the statues in the park. Streets did not hold interest. She followed Kevin's band into a hovel-hole. It was called *the Spartan* and it lived up to its name.

They squeezed the band equipment through a birth canal of a hallway and into a tiny, shabby place, full of people who all seemed to know everyone else in the small audience. No matter. Petra held the guitar, rigid and contained.

"Wish us luck," Kevin said, crouching from the stage to take the instrument. He paused, artfully, the breath catching audibly in his throat. "Your eyes…they're so blue."

"Thank you." They were gray. "Good luck."

He was a player, through and through. By that time, the groupies in *the Spartan* had noticed, had zeroed in on the possible scent of blood, like sharks circling.

"You and Kevin were getting comfortable," one of them growled over her un-lit cigarette.

"You could say so," Petra stated simply.

"He's leaving, you know. For the army." Another one, blonde, with heavy make-up, wearing black and denim.

"Yep." Their teeth couldn't poke holes in her.

"Shame he'll have to cut the hair." A third, dressed asymmetric and bright.

"Mm." Petra was noncommittal.

They drifted after that, sensing there was no blood in her rock-cold veins. They saw at once what she was. No one could dredge emotion from a stone.

And they were the same, same, same.

"Let's go get shots." Erin gripped her arm. Petra was instantly jealous. *Erin* was having a good time. *Erin* was having an adventure. Erin was warm and her skin was soft, smelling of sweat and apple perfume. "Jager good?"

Petra took a sip from the coffee cup. "Fabulous."

The band played uninspired punk, which was all she could expect. Throughout it, the dancing, the strobes, the claustrophobic darkness, Petra waited for something to happen.

"I've got to pee," Erin bumped her.

"Okay." Petra followed her. There was a girl with a bleeding foot in the bathroom, leaving cherry red kisses on the tile. Petra envied the life that girl was leading, the life inside of her.

Petra had nothing. She stayed at the mirror, assessing her own static self, the white of her cheeks, like polished marble. Her terrible dilemma, staying victorious, unbroken, but also bored.

Erin appeared from the stall.

"Mike is cute," Erin pronounced. Her face was flushed, she was having fun. "I think I'll try him next."

"Which one's Mike?"

"The driver."

When they came back, they discovered they had missed the last song.

"Did you like it?" Kevin asked, when the band was breaking down the set.

"Because when I give…I never really give at all," Petra quoted his previous lyrics back at him. It was what any artist wanted to hear – their own work mirrored by another, carved onto another soul. He was no different. Same, same, same.

Back outside into the air. Then back to the parking garage, regrettably shy of the witching hour. Dutifully, they had forgotten the level they'd parked at. Eventually, Petra swanned into the van, Kevin pursuing the space next to her.

"Smoke?"

"Sure."

"I've been waiting for this." He put an arm around her, claiming her, as if such a thing were possible. It was unclear if he was referring to the bowl or to her body. Strip-breathed, he handed her the pipe.

His other hand went up her shirt, like an animal sniffing at her base, tentative, tapping out its territory. He could claw at her all he wanted, he could not put one chink in her flesh.

He began to kiss her. Clinical vodka married to earthy smoke. The van's floor had more comfort than a city toilet, but the same amount of skeez. Petra placed her fingers on his fly, showing feigned interest. He responded, but nothing stirred within her.

"Gotta pee again," Erin said from somewhere.

"It's a long ride home," said someone else. The drummer, maybe. It didn't matter.

Same, same, same.

Petra was stone and would remain unbroken.

DRAMA

ANOTHER DOG BARKS, I BARK

SARAH BERGMAN

SCENE
(GRACE, stoic, kneels in the apartment. She blindly speaks to herself, unaware of the world around her.
ROBERT paces around her.)

Grace
Three plates. The first from my sister's fifth birthday, her handprints in the center. We glazed them over. Mine long gone, but hers still intact. When she died, I kept it. The second from a Goodwill downtown. Flowers around the edges. A favorite. The third was some plain old thing. Still mattered.

Robert
Grace.

Grace
Still mattered. A rug. A giant stain, a red wine stain, in the center of the carpet. Huge. It's a blob, almost like two handprints. I'll have to replace it.

Robert
Grace.

Grace
Don't interrupt, Robert. The shelf beside the front door. Where we put the picture frames, a scratch, I could forgive, but long splinters down the side and along the back. Six picture frames. Two small ones of my sister and me at her fourteenth birthday party. Of my mom. The rest, medium-sized. One of us at our wedding. One of us at the hotel in Atlanta. One of you when you got your doctorate. One of you holding a fish. The fish was bigger than you. I took the picture, and I loved the way the fish looked up at you like it needed air. Desperate. Eyes flashing around, wriggling. You let it go. All six frames smashed.

Grace's Mother
Hey! F—r! Yeah, you! Look at my daughter! Look at what you did!

Robert
Grace.

Grace
The coffee table. Out in the living room. Glass splashed all over the tile. The metal groaned. I can hear it. It rings in my ears, even now, Robert. I can still hear it.

Robert
Grace. Listen to me.

Grace's Mother
When you two got married, I let her let you wear a powder-blue tux at the wedding. At the time, I thought, "Oh, it's what Grace wants." Now I come to find that she wanted her wedding at a church, wanted her wedding in shades of dark purple, wanted her wedding to have a DJ with some good music taste, not bad R&B from the late nineties. But no! She let you play August Alsina. She let you wear powder-f—ing-blue! She let you
hold the wedding Jesus f—ing Christ, man, let her grieve!

Robert
Grace. Get up.

Grace's Mother
Let her grieve.

Grace
The kitchen counter has pieces chipped out. Like someone was mining for gold in the marble.

Robert
They're just things.

Grace
My things. Just things. The kitchen chairs. One of the cushions is ripped. Another is stained. The third is missing.

Grace's Mother
My daughter described you after the second date, saying you were a god. You're not God! You're a six-figure manipulative/no-good god. I hate you!

Grace
Where did the third one go?

Robert
It's over. Get up. The whole thing is over now. I'm not mad anymore.

Grace's Mother
Leave him.

Grace
The kitchen table has water burns all over it, the rings of a cup without a coaster circling random spots. The wood is ruined forever. Water burned into the wood, and it's ruined forever!

Robert
Water doesn't burn.

Grace's Mother
Hit her! Goddman you, man, she can't go to the police unless she has a wound. You're breaking things, but you won't even touch her!

Robert
Grace. I love you, Grace.

Grace
Six crystal glasses. From the wedding. One by one. I saw all the hairline cracks in the stems and still. Your mother gave them to us for the wedding. You were so nice when you showed me.

Grace's Mother
They were from Pier One, probably.

Grace
Carved flowers. Strong. Did you know, when I first saw them I loved them? Perfect weight. You could feel that they were heavy—one by one. You pulled them from the box and dropped them from the balcony.

Grace's Mother
No!

Robert
They're just things.

Grace
Yes. Just things. They cracked, one by one. Some at the stem, where the hairlines were. Some in the cup part. Whatever.

Robert
Gracie, come on. Let's make dinner.

Grace
Dinner. What would you like for dinner?

Robert
Let's make shrimp scampi.

Grace
Shrimp scampi. Okay. We can make that.

Robert
Grace, I love you.

Grace
I love / you too.

Grace's Mother
Robert, the first time I met you, I could still see the blood of other girls on your mouth. Easy. You were the type of guy who liked things. Cars and protein bars and under-pars and tiny but eventful scars. Loved showing stuff off. Loved showing off that watch you *scumbag.* I hate you. And then Gracie stopped calling on weekends after the gym. She loved the things you did, loved when things shone in the sun, and god, I hate you. I hate all of this. This is my child!

Grace
My mom says, hi.

Grace's Mother
I do not.

Robert
How is she?

Grace's Mother
I'm sick of my daughter ignoring me because you've locked her up in this stupid house.

Robert
Grace, get up. How is your mother?

Grace's Mother
She's crying every moment she has alone. In stairwells. On park benches. She's a bucket overflowing. You shove her down like a bad memory, every time, and she f—ing knows it!

Grace
Mom is feeling like six crystalline glasses—one by one. A coffee table smashed in. Plates smashed. Cushions ripped. She feels like blinds unspooled from each other. Cracked marble. Holes in the drywall. Paint peeling from ripping old adhesive from the ceiling.

Robert
And your dad? Grace, tell me about your dad.

Grace
My mom told me she guesses where north is. She let out the dogs the other day and just let them run, and run. And they didn't come back when it got dark. And they didn't come back at all.

Grace's Mother
Hey!

Grace
Weren't even her dogs, I don't think.

Robert
Let's make dinner.

Grace
How do you feel?

Robert
Me? How do I feel?

Grace
How do you feel?

Robert
I guess like.

Grace
Because I feel like six crystalline glasses. One by one. I am smashing onto the concrete.

Robert
No!

Grace
Like a window with no blinds and a brick. A big, hot-baked brick with plenty of backswing.

Robert
Get back!

Grace
A pregnancy test. One. Snapped in half. I hadn't even. Snapped in half.

Robert
Grace, calm down. Don't get hysterical.

Grace
I didn't know what the inside of a pregnancy test looked like. Blue. The inside of a pregnancy test is blue.

(beat)

Robert
Grace

Grace's Mother
Grace

Grace
My mom let the dogs go. They probably bit the heads off raccoons. They're probably on their way home, licking their chops and desperate for treats. Mom just let them go.

Grace's Mother
I let them.

Grace
And they ran. You never want anything that runs to run so quickly, because what if they get lost. What if they get lost and can't come home. What then, Robert?

Robert
I.

Grace
Mom called me. She told me she let them go. Did you know her voice sounded like music? Like crystalline glasses dropping from a balcony?

Robert
You're speaking nonsense. I have no idea what you're talking about.

Grace's Mother
Sometimes, when you let something go, that thing doesn't do what it's supposed to. You want it to do something. Circle around you with big puppy eyes. Bark. Not run. You don't want the thing to run. You want it to stay, and you can't make it stay.

Robert
She didn't have to let the dogs go. Is this really about dogs?

Grace
Sometimes, when you let something go, that thing doesn't do what it's supposed to. You drop a glass from the balcony, and instead of shattering…

Robert
Yes?

Grace's Mother
Instead of shattering, it runs.

Grace
It runs?

Robert
It runs?

Grace
Maybe not.

Robert
What are you talking about?

Grace
I don't know. When I watched you drop those glasses, I think what came to mind were the dogs. And how they could have done anything but run. Cry. Stay. Bark. But they bolted out.

Grace's Mother
They wanted to run.

Grace
Glasses don't want anything. They just hit the ground. They don't run.

Robert
Grace, are you saying you're glass?

Grace
Stop trying to make sense of what I'm saying, Robert.

Grace's Mother
Glass hits the ground.

Grace
I'm saying that they're not the same. Letting go, hoping to destroy. Letting go, hoping to keep. Letting go, hoping for.

Robert
This is silly.
(beat)
Grace
Yes. It is silly.

(GRACE stands up, finally, and exits)

Robert
Where are you going? Grace? Grace, where are you going?

Grace
I'm not glass.

(Dim lights. End of scene)

DE-EDEN'D SCENES

S. T. BRANT

Memory, the God of Limits

Argument:
The beginning of all things was Caprice and Calliope. Caprice first, and then Calliope. Caprice bloomed from naught, a flowerhead in the abyss that seeded later. Caprice, a singer, sang Life while Calliope sewed the shawl of Being around her melody. Calliope, in play, pricked with her stitching Caprice upon the hand; and Caprice unfurled the beginning word, her song being a hum and wordless song- Ow, followed by the laughter of Calliope at the discovery of pain. The undertow of Harmony: a memory of pain; the motive of Laughter: a comment on the Pain.

Memory, the god of limits, bloomed from a laugh in dark, a gloom itinerant to Nothing's burst
Caprice toward Life! but prolonged, an envy trenchant in that blank primordial;
Caprice and Calliope have a joy for one another though there's tucked a shadow in her,
Dark Calliope!
Joking, she pricked Caprice,
Something in her laughed not at the joke but at the prick:

Memory was born.
A joke, repeated, brings less joy,
Thus happiness: delimited.

Two Eden Scenes

i. To Have Lived Too Long in the Grave of Life

Adam, the eroticist, proposes multiplying; Eve proposes metaphysics.

Adam: We shall make the noise of the earth being made.
Eve: Think it came as singing? some melody duplicated from a prior being?
Was there harmony with Life- or discord?
Is that Discordia the living strain today?
If only they had harmonized, the creating things, caprices.

ii. Arcadia, Ego

The Fates lament their station.

Clotho: In even Eden we were poets, metaphoric…
Did we misstep? Always there was susceptibility to wind…tempests
In joy…

Lachesis: The authority of Authority displaces error. Our grievance is our secondness to god.
That all god's errors are ours,
That god, the confounder, blasts us that he's conscious,
That he strains, sees upon him stains.

Atropos: Plucking's eternalized all ruin.

Two Eve Scenes

i. Eve in Love

Eve reflects on Adam.

Our secrets are the tyrants of our souls;
They flail the innocence of our relations;
They assail our assignment of an appraisal.

Time makes infelicitous our love;
We are loved for what we have become,
But what we've done…- Love would never have begun.

ii. On Gardening

Scene: Eve wanders through Eden and foresees the end.

Now and Always: a sadness will core Joy
That Sadness pities-
Our hearts' despair, our hearts' demise: our hearts!
Ecstasy! bleed
The rage you yell that tunes satyrs childing in discord.

Wretched penury of chaos,

Tree of dreams,

I scooped from Tigris and felt the Atlas of another Eden.

Pick a flower: Atlas to a gentler world- then
Feel a flower to an... excess, Might.

A Song

A group gathers around a large campfire. Eden burning. Discussing the lapsarian legend there is mentioned Love and Fault and Why. Someone, an older participant in the crowd, cowled (from cold?) addresses them inlay:

Eros sees the sky, the sun in all its Might.

Eden is composed of Love, We are notes of Music;
O, we soften our prestige when we exemplify the brutish;
Love? love? a bird in flight by fluke,
One wing hoisted on vacuumed loot,
The other a ruin'd light, ruin's music.

Eros apostates to Autumn, the day is fallen.

Was the Tree of Love eaten from? unknown. Eden's bones.
We'll assume. We'll lie.
Let there be belief there's a romance in our lineal notes.
Love dies.
There's blood but in our blood: Adam fancied the Tree of Power.
Eve's fault? Adam failed to bite from Love!
Why not sing Eve's starvation? That's a sadder song.

Eros wanders winter night, warms herself at firesides, sings her heartache into light.

The Everyday of Gods

i. Subvert the Trope for Father

The mythos: Caprice, chaos, the incipience of Life and first Power, is carefree of that fact; all other gods (Time; God; etc.) curse the timing of their being...

God's belated anxiety argues for Time being the progenitor of All; Time, being attributed a quality of god's, claims Time started before Caprice- will *cede* simultaneity.

Cari declines to worry about priority, her's is implicit in her.

Life, striving for Caprice, contrives for *Life* through detachment of the mother from the end of all things, Time, and makes Cari the beginning who never desires an end.

We strive toward beginnings that beget more beginnings, against the father whose power is to end but not beget. Time and Life: true Life defeats Time.

ii. Life Envies Nothing's Fullness!

God begins the poem; god ends.

What I am: what you say.
Someone new will proclaim me something else,
Which I'll become,
Yet I won't remain what you have me-
There's more to know!

Conscience-stricken still! God, the god of guilt. Infinity's prolonged...
Its wick's burn paused.
Proclaim it what it was, that rustle through the terebinths...
The loss of god.

Outtakes from *Genesis*

i.
The Scene:
An exchange takes place between a Theban (a city concomitant with Eden)- who blames the loss of Thebes on the loss of Eden- and Eve, unbeknownst to the Theban.

T: What differs Thebes from Eden that it was perfect in its privileges?
Why Eden? Was some resident salvation restrained inside that exclusive cage?
Was some remedy to all of this incubate in Eden?
E: Nothing.
Then Eden failed!

Since its birth. Since Eve's vacation.
I can feel the misery of all evicted; I can feel the fire from the garden;
I can see it flamed to kill the blight-
T (becoming aware that he talks to Eve): Perfect's sick, so are the perfect sick.
I sadly queen'd some other lands.
Did others follow you from Eden?
That pain about your bones is the contagiousness of Suffering's home.

ii.
The Scene:
Adam is asked if he knew Adam by a party curious about recent events. Adam is unrecognized and reveals that he and Eve have parted ways since Eden. He laughs about his namesake and perseveres wandering.

Did you?
-Well.
Where's he?
-Wandering.
And Eve?
-Passed.
Shame. The cause?
-Necessity crossed her.
You are?
-Adamah. – *I laugh and leave.*

WINGS

KRISTA DEBEHNKE

DELILAH
DR. BRANCH
(Fade in. Stage is a simple doctor's office. CS is a chaise lounge and a leather armchair, facing each other. DR. BRANCH is sitting in the armchair. Between the chaise lounge and armchair is a coffee table with books, a clipboard, a pen, and a pitcher of water with glasses. DR. BRANCH looks at her watch and stands, crosses to SL.)

DR. BRANCH

(calling)

Delilah? I'm ready for you, now.

DELILAH

(entering from SL)

Okay.

(DR. BRANCH and DELILAH sit.)

DR. BRANCH

I'd like for us to spend a few minutes checking in.

DELILAH

(thinking)

Checking in.

DR. BRANCH

Yes. How have you been feeling?

DELILAH

Okay, I guess.

DR. BRANCH

That's good.

DELILAH

(pause)

It's weird. I always think about what I want to say to you before I get here, and then when I get here, it all flies away.

DR. BRANCH

Why do you think that is?

DELILAH

I don't know. Maybe I want someone to understand what goes on in my head exactly when it happens... and not force me to tell them.

DR. BRANCH

You want someone to read your mind. Is that it?

DELILAH

Not exactly. Just what I want them to know.

DR. BRANCH

And what do you want them to know?

DELILAH

It's not necessarily about want. It's about need.

DR. BRANCH

Oh? That's a little more serious.

DELILAH

Well, yes. It's a serious situation.

DR. BRANCH

Are you referring to what we discussed last week?

DELILAH

Always.

DR. BRANCH

Would you say that's a reoccurring thought for you?

DELILAH

Does something reoccur if it never leaves? Isn't that more constant?

DR. BRANCH

Perhaps it is.

DELILAH

You can't stop thinking about something that never leaves you. It's a part of me... a part of my body.

DR. BRANCH

That sounds very hard for you.

DELILAH

(suddenly angry)

You're damn right it is! Why don't you try being me— a freak!

DR. BRANCH

There is nothing freakish about you, Delilah.

DELILAH

Are you sure? How can you be sure?

DR. BRANCH

I'm looking right at you. What I see is a young woman whose brain is not always so kind to her.

DELILAH

(accusing)

What about my body?

DR. BRANCH

(in a kind voice)

What about your body?

DELILAH

These—

(clawing at her shoulder blades)

These THINGS!

DR. BRANCH

This is just a manifestation of your fear, Delilah. There's nothing there.

DELILAH

But I feel them! I can see them!

DR. BRANCH

No matter how many times I reassure you that you're okay—

DELILAH

(mocking)

It's no use—

DR. BRANCH

It's no use because you've already created this pathway in your mind. Once you think there's something there, you start to believe it. What therapy does is it retrains your brain to think differently. To see yourself without— what was it?

DELILAH

It's WINGS! There are wings growing out of me!

DR. BRANCH

Wings. That's right.

(beat)

What do wings represent to you? What memories do you recall having to do with wings?

DELILAH

It's a parasite feeding off of me.

DR BRANCH

A parasite? Let's hold onto that thought for a little while.

DELILAH

A parasite that invaded my body... these aren't the happy, light wings of a hummingbird. These wings are heavy, like— like lifting a wet blanket over your shoulder. Sopping. Uncomfortable.

DR. BRANCH

When did you first see the wings?

DELILAH

It was sudden.

DR. BRANCH

One day they were just there?

DELILAH

No, it was more of a process. I started to feel bumps beneath my shoulder blades. Both soft and hard, like ear cartilage.

DR. BRANCH

Then what?

DELILAH

We went to the doctor, who found nothing. Not surprising.

DR. BRANCH

Hmmm.

DELILAH

Then, it happened. I was changing my shirt in front of my stand-up mirror, and I turned around to see— them.

DR. BRANCH

What happened?

DELILAH

They broke through the skin. It felt like being pricked with a needle at first, but eventually they ripped my skin right open, gnawing teeth cracking my fragile egg-skin. They were there, like two ugly baby birds, black and wet with the moisture of my body, blood and whatever else, just hanging there on my back.

(beat)

I remember— I remember turning side to side. And the more I cried out, the more they seemed to live.

DR. BRANCH

What do you mean, "live"?

DELILAH

It's like they enjoyed it. They liked hearing me cry.

DR. BRANCH

What a terrifying moment for you.

DELILAH

(beat)

Do you ever say anything helpful?

DR. BRANCH

What would be helpful for you right now?

DELILAH

(sarcastic)

Oh, I don't know. Maybe acknowledge that there are literal bird wings growing on my back?

DR. BRANCH

I don't see anything, Delilah.

DELILAH

They crawl back inside sometimes.

DR. BRANCH

Why do you think that is?

DELILAH

I don't know. It's like they don't want anyone but me to see them.

DR. BRANCH

Have you tried showing others?

DELILAH

My mom, you know. We talked about this last week.

DR. BRANCH

And that's why you're here, seeing me? She didn't believe you?

DELILAH

No.

DR. BRANCH

If you could, what would you say your wings want?

DELILAH

Me.

DR. BRANCH

They want you? How do you mean?

DELILAH

They want to take me. To destroy me.

DR. BRANCH

Why would they want to destroy you?

DELILAH

Beats me.

DR. BRANCH

I don't think this is healthy, Delilah.

DELILAH

Of course it's not! I'm— I'm part bird!

DR. BRANCH

You're not part bird. You're a young woman who has personified her grief into something physical—

DELILAH

Personification? That's what you're calling it?

DR. BRANCH

I can't, as a medical professional, agree that you have wings that show up and disappear whenever they please. From a medical standpoint, it seems as if you've imagined—

DELILAH

Imagined!

DR. BRANCH

(talking over DELILAH)

—Imagined your pain, perhaps the pain of your past, or something bothering you presently— into something you could visualize. Like wings.

DELILAH

Do you think I like this "visualization?" Dr. Branch?

DR. BRANCH

Of course not.

DELILAH

Do you think I like standing in front of the mirror and watching my Frankenstein's Monster body transform into something—unrecognizable?

DR. BRANCH

Delilah, listen—

DELILAH

Listening gets me nowhere. Nobody believes me. Nobody sees this part of me.

DR. BRANCH

What would you do if someone could see them?

DELILAH

Then I would be free.

DR. BRANCH

What is free?

(long pause. DELILAH fidgets in her seat.)

Delilah? Are you okay?

(DELILAH suddenly jumps up and tries to grab at her back. DR. BRANCH jumps up and reaches towards DELILAH.)

DELILAH

Don't! Touch! Me!

(DELILAH twists and writhes on her feet.)

This feels different.

(DR. BRANCH takes a few steps backward, awed. DELILAH rips at her shirt and moves CS. Two wings emerge from beneath her shirt, black, and erect, like the wings of an airplane.)

DR. BRANCH

Wings.

DELILAH

(beat)

Wings.

(DELILAH smiles. Blackout.)

THE END

BILL OF HEALTH

WILLIAM IVOR FOWKES

CHARACTERS:

LAWRENCE FENTON. Male. A patient.
(Age 100 in Scene One; 70 in Scene Two; 40 in Scene Three.)

DR. COREY RIPLEY. Any Gender. Lawrence's primary care physician.
(Age 85 in Scene One; 55 in Scene Two; 25 in Scene Three.)

TIME: 2045 (Scene One); 2015 (Scene Two); 1985 (Scene Three)

PLACE: A doctor's office in Manhattan.

SET: 2 chairs and a desk.

SCENE ONE: The year 2045. LAWRENCE meets with his doctor.

DR. RIPLEY
Blood pressure, normal. Blood sugar level, good. HIV negative, of course. Cholesterol, very healthy. Liver, kidney, thyroid—all good. All phenomenal, in fact.

LAWRENCE
Big deal.

DR. RIPLEY
Good health at your age *is* a big deal! Look—when I set out to become a doctor, I never dreamed I'd have patients like you. You're a medical miracle, Lawrence!

LAWRENCE
Come off it! I don't feel any different from last year—or any other year.

DR. RIPLEY
That's my point. You turn 100 next month—what a milestone! Yet you're still carrying on like a man half your age. And you don't look a day over 40!

LAWRENCE
Now I know you're joking.

DR. RIPLEY
OK, maybe 50. But at this rate, you'll probably live another 20 years, maybe even much longer.

LAWRENCE

(sadly)

I never asked for this.

DR. RIPLEY
But isn't this what everyone wants?

LAWRENCE
How would *you* like to be left behind? My best friends are all gone—as you well know. My husband died ten years ago. I have no family left.

I'm the only surviving member of my college class. I don't even get to go to reunions anymore.

DR. RIPLEY
Well, whether you like it or not, I'm afraid you're a very healthy man and destined to remain so for years to come. That means my work is done here.

LAWRENCE
What are you saying?

DR. RIPLEY
I mean I'm retiring. My wife and I are moving to North Carolina next month.

LAWRENCE
Why in the world would you do that?

DR. RIPLEY
I've got a lot of reading and golfing to catch up on.

LAWRENCE
What about your responsibility to your patients? To me?

DR. RIPLEY
I take that very seriously. That's why I'm turning you over to Dr. Evelyn Grossman. She was voted one of the city's 10 best doctors by *New York Magazine.*

LAWRENCE
But we've been through so much together. You're the only person left who knew me in the dark old days.

DR. RIPLEY
Yes, I know. And it's been a privilege to know you and watch you become the magnificent and healthy man you are today.

LAWRENCE
And you're too young to retire!

DR. RIPLEY
I'm 85, Lawrence. It's time. While you may have stopped aging, most of the rest of us have been steadily marching toward decrepitude. I just don't have the energy to keep doing this.

LAWRENCE
That settles it then.

DR. RIPLEY
Settles what?

LAWRENCE
Now don't get upset, Corey, but I've given this idea a lot of thought.

DR. RIPLEY
What idea?

LAWRENCE
I don't want to live any longer. I want you to help me die.

DR. RIPLEY
I'll do no such thing!

LAWRENCE
All I want is one of those pills. I know all about them. Only doctors can get them. Just get me one for old times' sake. I won't tell anyone where I got it.

DR. RIPLEY
You won't be able to if you're dead.

LAWRENCE

Seriously. Please give me one of those pills. I'm begging you.

DR. RIPLEY
Sorry, I won't do that.

LAWRENCE
Suit yourself, but with or without your help, I'm going to kill myself.

Lawrence storms out.

SCENE TWO: The year 2015. LAWRENCE meets with his doctor.

DR. RIPLEY
Another great checkup, Lawrence. And I've saved the best for last—your HIV test results. We've never used the word "cured" when it comes to AIDS and HIV, but your viral levels are now so beyond "untraceable" it's undeniable. You're the first documented patient ever to be cured—completely cured—of this dreadful disease. Congratulations!

LAWRENCE
(glumly)
Big deal.

DR. RIPLEY
Don't you understand? When you were first diagnosed, I didn't think you'd survive ten years. But to make it to 70 and to be completely cured? It's a medical phenomenon!

LAWRENCE
Hey, does this mean others will be completely cured now, too?

DR. RIPLEY
That's the big question. We don't know why you've been cured. We need to find other people with your results and then dig deeper. But after so many years of treatments—and I remember all too well how

rough things were for you in the early days—you can finally rest easy. I'm so happy for you.

LAWRENCE
Who else knows about this?

DR. RIPLEY
Just the staff here and a couple of my colleagues. But when I submit my journal article, the whole medical community will know.

LAWRENCE
You can't publish an article. I don't want anyone to know about this.

DR. RIPLEY
I don't understand.

LAWRENCE
Listen, you know my best friends are all HIV-positive, right?

DR. RIPLEY
Yes, of course. I treat many of them.

LAWRENCE
So you know our situation. We're the lucky ones—the survivors. But it's been no picnic. Our activities have been limited; we've taken tons of pills, and whenever one of us has gotten sick, there have been horrible complications. But what's made it bearable is knowing that we're all in this together. We're a community. Now this news could jeopardize all that.

DR. RIPLEY
Wouldn't they be happy for you?

LAWRENCE
Maybe, but things would never be the same. That fundamental bond

between us would be broken, and I'd be pushed out, left behind. So, promise me you won't publish your article. Please, Corey!

DR. RIPLEY
Lawrence, this is bigger than you and me. The whole world needs to hear this. And, besides, I wouldn't identify you by name. I never identify my patients.

LAWRENCE
People would figure it out. My friends all know you're my doctor. And I'm sure there are reporters out there who'd find a way.

DR. RIPLEY
I think you're being paranoid.

LAWRENCE
And I never gave you permission to put my information out there!

DR. RIPLEY
Well, actually, you did. You signed a waiver when you first came to see me.

LAWRENCE stands up abruptly.

LAWRENCE
If you publish that article, Dr. Ripley—I'll sue you!

Lights down.

SCENE THREE: The year 1985. LAWRENCE meets with his new doctor.

DR. RIPLEY
Nice to meet you, Mr. Fenton. May I ask why you've changed doctors?

LAWRENCE
My doctor died.

DR. RIPLEY
Sorry to hear it. Was he old?

LAWRENCE
32.

DR. RIPLEY
Oh, my. Was it AIDS?

LAWRENCE
Yes.

DR. RIPLEY
Sad. Very sad.

LAWRENCE
They're dying all around us.

DR. RIPLEY
Yes, it's tragic. And now Rock Hudson, too. I just hope this finally pushes Reagan to start funding AIDS research. But let's talk about you. I've reviewed everything, and I'm very impressed. Blood pressure, normal. Blood sugar level, good. Cholesterol, very healthy. Liver, kidney, thyroid—all good. HIV negative. In short, you're in excellent health for a man of 40. But I'm concerned that you haven't been getting regular checkups—especially in the midst of this crisis. It's been over two years. Why have you waited so long?

LAWRENCE
I've been busy.

DR. RIPLEY
We're all busy. What have you been doing?

LAWRENCE
Helping people die.

DR. RIPLEY
Oh, you mean you've been doing volunteer work?

LAWRENCE
I don't consider it "work." And I never volunteered for it—it's just something I have to do. You see.. well, I lost my partner a year ago. We were together for 22 years.

DR. RIPLEY
I'm so sorry.

LAWRENCE
No one in college even knew we were anything more than friends. Hell, the APA still considered it a mental illness back then. But after graduation, we moved to New York and became the out-est, proudest, bad-est couple of queens you ever saw. We thought we'd always be together—and always be surrounded by our friends. But now he's dead. And my friends and coworkers are all dying, too. So, I've got to take care of them before they're all gone, and I'm the only one left behind.

DR. RIPLEY
That's very admirable. Now, I hope you're taking all the proper precautions.

LAWRENCE
What do you mean?

DR. RIPLEY
Do you scrub down after each visit? Are you careful about what you touch? Do you avoid all contact with bodily fluids? That sort of thing?

LAWRENCE
No, I don't.

DR. RIPLEY
But you've got to! There's a lot we don't know about this dreadful disease yet.

LAWRENCE
It is dreadful, yes.

DR. RIPLEY
And as your doctor, I have to ask you—are you sexually active?

LAWRENCE
As active as I can be.

DR. RIPLEY
What does that mean?

LAWRENCE
I'm not going to let this plague defeat me or make me ashamed of being gay. And I like sex. I'm not afraid to admit it. Being intimate with other men is part of what connects me to my community.

DR. RIPLEY
That's all fine, but do you practice safe sex?

LAWRENCE
I don't like condoms.

DR. RIPLEY
Okay, so you abstain from anal intercourse?

LAWRENCE
No.

DR. RIPLEY
You do realize that we think anal intercourse is the primary means of transmission of HIV?

LAWRENCE
Yes, I do.

DR. RIPLEY
Then you have no choice—you have to use condoms or else abstain.

LAWRENCE
I do have a choice. I choose to be unsafe.

DR. RIPLEY
That makes no sense.

LAWRENCE
Neither does AIDS.

DR. RIPLEY
Yes, but…

LAWRENCE
Look, I told you I don't want to be left behind.

DR. RIPLEY
But what you're doing is dangerous!

LAWRENCE
It's my choice.

DR. RIPLEY
But it's an absurd choice!

LAWRENCE
It's what I want to do.

DR. RIPLEY
But it's suicidal!

LAWRENCE
Yes, I know.

END OF PLAY

A MORE PERFECT UNION

KIM KOLARICH

<u>Characters</u>
Rebecca: 20-30 years old, female
Cody: 20-30 years old, male
Lynn: 30 years old, male

<u>Setting</u>
A restaurant.

<u>Time</u>
1999, 2010, 2014, 2016.

LIGHTS UP

(The year is 1999. A restaurant. A table with two chairs. CODY sits and sips a glass of water. He adjusts the menu across from him, then quickly reads his menu. He smooths his hair, then puts a red rose he has brought with him into his glass of water. As he looks around, REBECCA approaches the table.)

REBECCA
You must be Cody.

(CODY looks up and is pleased to see her.)

CODY
Yeah. Yeah, I am. I know that you're Rebecca, then because I'm Cody. If I'm Cody, then you're Rebecca because I'm supposed to meet a Rebecca. Who happens to be you.

REBECCA
(Laughing)
Get out much?

CODY
Actually, I do ¾

REBECCA
Can I sit down, then?

CODY
Of course.
(He quickly stands and pulls the chair out for her.)

REBECCA
I saw the rose when I came in.

CODY
Good eye.

REBECCA
Well, you can't miss it. It's the only table with a flower in here.

CODY
Yeah, it is. Isn't it?
(He goes to hand her the flower but realizes the stem is dripping with water, so he shakes it but accidentally drops it. They both lean over and pick it up at the same time. Rebecca puts it on the table.)

REBECCA
Thank you. Did you realize a red rose symbolizes courage and respect?

CODY
Ah, well, that's all they had at the store. I didn't want to bring you an ugly-ass petunia or something¾

REBECCA
Well, thanks. I like this restaurant.

CODY
I've never been here. But the food looks good. I was scanning the menu¾

REBECCA
Thanks for letting me pick the place.

CODY
You know... Shelia described you, but I didn't think you'd look like... like you do¾

REBECCA
Okay...

CODY
It's just that you're so pretty...

REBECCA
She didn't say that I have a great personality?

CODY
No. I mean, yes. She did say that…but not a lot else. She just thought we'd get along well.

REBECCA
Because we both liked "The Blair Witch Project"?

CODY
Man. It scared the sh-t out of me!

REBECCA
When James gets killed?!

CODY
Why would anybody go into the woods? What's wrong with the beach? A nice wide-open beach? With no trees. Just sand.
(They laugh. REBECCA picks up her menu.)

REBECCA
I always get the hamburgers here. They're topped with avocados¾

CODY
Avocado on a hamburger?

REBECCA
You never know until you try it.

CODY
Ah, okay. I'll get whatever you're getting.

(They close the menus. CODY smiles at her.)

CODY
So are you afraid of everything going haywire¾

REBECCA
What? On my hamburger?

CODY

No, I mean with the clocks changing from 1999 to 2000? Y2K.

REBECCA
Oh, that. No. What for?

CODY
Really? The end of a century coming to an end, and you're not afraid that 2000 won't be indistinguishable from, say, 1900?

REBECCA
Well, I certainly can tell the difference.

CODY
Most clocks are run on computers and isn't it automatically assumed that all time begins with a 19? You know... for years that is. Don't you think everything that keeps time will shut down completely? I mean, maybe a little bit? (Pause.) Maybe just one clock? Toss me a bone. How 'bout your watch?

REBECCA
Well, everything's fixable.

CODY
Is that your final answer?

REBECCA
Final answer.

LIGHTS OUT

LIGHTS UP
(The year is 2001. At lights up CODY and REBECCA sit down at the same restaurant table and look over the menu.)

REBECCA

Why do we keep coming here?

CODY
You love this place. You're keeping the avocado farms in business.

REBECCA
That's no reason to keep coming back. I guess I'll get my usual.

CODY
I'll get it too.

REBECCA
(She looks at him.) Why have you been so nervous all night?

CODY
I'm not nervous.

REBECCA
Yes you are. Whenever you're nervous you order the same thing as me.

CODY
Then I'll get the turkey club. (Pause.) Do you know where Afghanistan is?

REBECCA
Well, I know it's not next door...And ah, well, I could find it on a map...wouldn't want to vacation there and get stuck next to bin Laden in my beach cabana. If you know what I mean.

CODY
I'm enlisting. (Pause.) I'm gonna to serve our country and get those f—rs.

REBECCA

Whoa! How did we go from a turkey club to becoming a soldier? You can't be serious.

CODY

I'm one hundred percent serious. I'm gonna do it. I've never felt so right about something in my life.

REBECCA

What about school? You have one year left. You can't just go off and leave. You're acting crazy.

CODY

I've gotta be crazy to let al-Qaeda fly another one of our jets into¾

REBECCA

That's not funny.

CODY

I'm serious, Becca.

REBECCA

Why do you have to say that?! Today was like the first day that I didn't think about it. I can still smell the smoke. Did you know that? (Pause.) You can't go anywhere. You won't be safe. I don't need you to do anything for me except stay here.

CODY

I can't sit by and let our country be a target. Imagine if every able man enlisted? It would be a different country. Terrorism wouldn't exist¾

REBECCA

(Panicking)

You can even date other people if you stay. Anything. The poker group you wanted to join? Done. That thingy where you and your friends go to bond¾

CODY
The guys' weekend in Vegas?

REBECCA
Done. Bonding done. Just go do it. I'll watch football with you. Anything. The fishing thing. Done. A blow job while driving? Easy. Done. Just don't go. Don't do this.

CODY
I can be a part of our national security. I can really do something. I can right the wrong.

REBECCA
National security? Who talks like that? (Pause.) You don't have to go. Cody! I saw it on the news. Didn't you see it on the news? The U.S. took down al Qaeda in Afghanistan. They kicked

REBECCA (cont'd)
them out of Kabul. And bin Laden is a cave dweller now. He's like in Pakistan. In some cave. It's done. He can't do anything from a cave. Cody, you're not going to join the marines or
whatever and risk your life to find somebody hiding out in a cave who doesn't have enough fashion sense to take the towel off his head when he gets out of the shower. Are you?

CODY
I gotta do this.

REBECCA
What? Did George Bush call you personally or something? I don't get this. What about us? What abo… me? You can't leave me.

CODY
This is about you. I'll be protecting your county… our country from terrorism. The marines are the single greatest weapon the U.S. has¾

REBECCA
(Begins to cry a little)
You sound like the brochure. I found your stupid marines' brochure, Cody. You left it in the sports section of the paper, you know.

CODY
Since when do you read the sports section?

REBECCA
Yeah, well, maybe I'm changing. You're not the only one who can change around here.

LIGHTS OUT

LIGHTS UP
(The year is 2010. At lights up CODY and REBECCA sit down at the same restaurant table and look over the menu. REBECCA puts the menu down.)

REBECCA
I'm not hungry.

CODY
Oh, come on, sweetie. This is your favorite place.

REBECCA
No, it's not.

CODY
Yes it is.

REBECCA
No, it's not.

CODY

Okay, it isn't.

REBECCA
Yes, it is. (Pause.) Another tour of duty? Really, Cody? You did your tour and you made it back alive. Isn't that good enough? You really called your commander and volunteered?

CODY
I gotta go back, Rebecca. (Pause.) I miss the food there.

REBECCA
Not funny.

CODY
Please, Becca. You have to understand this. Obama's got it right… to do this surge with more troops. We'll get bin Laden this time.

REBECCA
Well, just have our president send somebody else. And I saw on the news that this is the longest war the U.S. has ever been in. Did you know that?

CODY
You think I don't know that?

REBECCA
Why do we need to be there any longer? It's not working. Is nobody aware of this? Are Obama and Biden too busy watching reruns of Jersey Shore or something? This is insanity. Please don't go back.

CODY
I gotta go back… because I'm good at it.

REBECCA
What? Wow. (She gestures between them.) You're not good at this?

CODY
I never told you this before, but when I was deployed the last time, I showed this kid a photo of 9/11¾

REBECCA
You did not¾

CODY
The kid thought it was their capital, Kabul, in the photo.

REBECCA
Then why go back? If the people don't even understand what you're doing there¾

CODY
I have to go back. It's what I do. The Taliban is still there fighting us, and the Northern Alliance… we gotta get bin Laden and then provide a presence there. We can't leave it the way
it is¾

REBECCA
You're not a part of the we that started the war¾

CODY
We were called to the hospital¾

REBECCA
Please not now. Please don't tell me. I'm gonna be sick¾

CODY
To remove a local dead civilian¾

REBECCA
Stop, Cody. It's not my responsibility to hear your stories.

CODY
We have to if they die in our hospital. (Pause.) It turned out to be a three-year-old girl who was shot by the Taliban. (Pause.) Her father followed us to the morgue. We had to get his permission to take her into our care, you know, because we don't have any women in our platoon ¾

REBECCA
I'm pregnant¾

CODY
We put her in a handmade casket with an Afghanistan flag on it, draped over it...what did you say?

REBECCA
About six weeks along.

LIGHTS OUT

LIGHTS UP
(The year is 2014. At lights up LYNN and REBECCA sit down at the same restaurant table and look over the menu.)

REBECCA
What kind of a name is Lynn? I mean, for a like a guy? (Pause.) I'm sorry. That was rude. But when Sheila showed me your photo... I thought...I can overlook your ultra-feminine name, and I hoped that you might show up with...I don't know... with a hairy chest and eating a turkey leg and you'd have a black eye ¾
LYNN
You're funny. Lynn is an old family name. I'm glad you wanted to meet me. Shelia said we might get along. And thanks for picking out the restaurant.

REBECCA
Ah, no problem. Sometimes it can even be my favorite restaurant.

LYNN
Really? Great. I looked at the menu on-line and I think I might get the burger with the avocado topping.

REBECCA
Yeah. That's kinda getting old for me. I've ordered it in the past. Anywho. So you're a tax accountant?

LYNN
That's correct.

REBECCA
(Jokingly)
Well…it must be a dangerous profession.

LYNN
Actually, it is. Especially around April. As you know, that's tax season in America. Some people don't know how to clamp down on their cash flow during the year or don't know their break-even point if they own their own business or their overall value or how are they even going to pay their taxes. Are they paying too much? Or not enough? Will Uncle Sam come knocking on their door? Knock, knock. I'm dodging bullets all day long. That is for my clients. It's a figure
of speech. I mean, it's not really dangerous, I mean, for instance, say terms of going into real combat. But it comes close. Sheila didn't tell me what you do¾

REBECCA
I'm a mom.

LYNN
Oh. (Pause.) She, ah, didn't tell me you have a child¾

REBECCA

Yeah, it's kinda like going to war. I mean, battling with a toddler. Right?

LYNN
Oh, right. Yeah, they can be a handful. And… ah, your husband? You have a husband, then? Shelia didn't tell me that you were¾

REBECCA
He's out of the picture.

LYNN
You're divorced?

REBECCA
Sort of. I mean, no. I mean… have you heard of Afghanistan?

LYNN
Of course.

REBECCA
He's dead. He died there. He was in the military.

LYNN
Rebecca. I'm very sorry. What an honorable person¾

REBECCA
Don't worry, Lynn. You'll still get to do my taxes.

LYNN
Oh, I wasn't concerned about that.

REBECCA
It was a joke. (Pause.) I do my own taxes.

LYNN
(Realizing)

Oh, funny. You're funny. But I'm still sorry for your loss.

REBECCA
It's okay. I mean, it's not. But it's what he does. I mean, what he did. (Pause.) Why don't we order some food.... and then you can tell me more about you. I'd like that.

LIGHTS FADE OUT

WAITING FOR THE GODOTS

ROBIN SCHLAHT

Synopsis:

While waiting for friends to join them for dinner, a couple discuss… everyday things: buffet vs. a la carte, easy-to-clean furniture, and whether or not they still love one another.

ACT ONE, SCENE ONE
(An empty stage except for a SIGN reading "Please Wait to be Seated." SHE and HE ENTER, HE glancing at his watch. They stop near the sign.)

HE
Okay. Well. Five minutes.

SHE looks at him.

SHE
What?

HE
We're five minutes late.

SHE
Well, they were late last time. Very late.

HE
That's them, isn't it? With the blue shirt.

SHE
Where?

HE
In the middle.

SHE
No. No, never. Not even close. The Godots aren't here. Again.

HE
They're busy.

SHE
Doing what?

HE
Here. They're busy here. The restaurant.

SHE
Yes.

HE
That's a good thing. The buffet will be fresh. Replenished.

SHE
You're having the buffet?

HE
Thinking about it. You're not?

SHE
No. I wasn't planning to, no.

SHE looks around.

SHE (CONT'D)
There's a table.

SHE starts to move toward it.

HE
No, the sign says 'Wait to be Seated'.

SHE
Why? Come on. We'd be doing them a favor.

HE
No. We should wait.

SHE
We've been waiting five minutes already.

HE looks at his watch.

HE
Not even two minutes. And there's a system in place, obviously. Why fight it?

SHE
Well, it's not a very good system. That's clearly an available table for four. Let's take it.

HE
Ah, there. See? That waitress just gave us a nice smiling nod, with her "one minute please" finger in the air. It won't be long.

(SHE is dejected.)

SHE
Buffet in the evening seems strange. It's more of a lunchtime thing, isn't it? When you're in a hurry.

HE
Buffet or not, it's still the best curry in town.

SHE
And they water down the buffet, like adding tomato soup to the butter chicken.

HE
What? No. That's silly. The buffet is like a sampler for the a la carte.

SHE
Maybe, if they did only a lunchtime buffet, then it becomes a sort of recruitment tool for their full price a la carte evening service. But here, their buffet competes all day with their menu, so it's got to be the cheaper, lesser quality option.

HE
Go ahead. Say it.

SHE
What?

HE
For cheapskates. That's what you're really saying. For cheapskates. Like me.

SHE
No. No. Not necessarily. Not only for cheapskates. For gluttons also.

HE
Oh. Well...I suppose, for large appetites, yes, okay. But it's also a convenient sampler for people who want to experience a variety of dishes. Cost efficiently.

SHE
Or eat an enormous amount. Cost efficiently.

HE
Well, anyway, I'm going to partake of the deluxe flavor sampler experience.

SHE
You mean the watered-down pig trough experience.

HE
Okay, you order the butter chicken, and we'll compare it with my butter chicken from the buffet. To compare only. Don't be picking off my buffet plate. If they see you do that, they'll charge us for another buffet.

SHE
Don't be goofy.

HE
They will. Absolutely. I've seen it. Four teenage girls ordered three buffets, and the fourth only had a samosa or something, and she mooched off the other girls' plates. And when the bill arrived, they were charged for four buffets.

SHE
Well, I wouldn't mooch.

HE
And they couldn't pay, they didn't have enough money. The manager was going to call the police.

SHE
Was that here?

HE
No, it was Raja Palace.

SHE
What ended up happening?

HE
Ahhh… nothing.

SHE
Oh.

HE
I paid for the fourth buffet.

SHE
What? You paid?

HE
I couldn't… it was so… I couldn't enjoy my lunch with all the ruckus. It was easier just to help them pay. The manager was being an ass. I haven't been back there since. And the food is way better here.

SHE
I suppose.

HE
Worth the wait.

SHE
Well, worth one more minute, then we're sitting down.

HE
One minute? Come on, be reasonable.

SHE
One and a half.

HE
Mmm.

(HE looks at his watch.)

HE (CONT'D)
They're probably having sex.

SHE
What?

HE
The Godots.

SHE
Why would you say that?

HE
I don't know.

SHE
Is that what you imagine? Is that what you picture in your head when you think about the Godots? Them having sex?

HE
No. I don't know. It just came to mind. It's a possibility.

SHE
Do you picture them 69-ing? Or are they doing it doggy style in your head. Or--

HE
(interrupting)
Shhh... No... They're not... doing it in my head.

SHE
Right.

(They pause. HE looks at his watch. SHE looks at him looking at his watch.)

SHE (CONT'D)
Okay now you've got them doing it in my head.

HE
Really?

SHE
Let's change the subject.

HE
Okay.

(Pause, both thinking.)

HE (CONT'D)
I should text them--

SHE
(interrupting)
If they're doing it they're probably doing it in their living room, on that big white leather sectional thingy.

HE
Oh yeah.

SHE
Right? Why else would you have a big white leather sectional thingy?

HE
Yeah.

SHE
Lots of possibilities, positionally.

HE
Right.

SHE
Lots of possibilities.

HE
And easy to clean.

SHE
Exactly.

(They both picture the possibilities.)

HE
Maybe we should get one.

SHE
Hmm?

HE
A big white leather sectional thingy.

SHE
No. Why?

HE
Umm... Well, we could... They're so easy to clean.

SHE
No. No. What we have is fine.

HE
No, you're right.

SHE
We're not really a big white leather sectional thingy sort of couple.

HE
Yeah, I guess..I guess not.

(They pause.)

SHE
They're probably having an argument, is what they're having.

HE
Is that what you picture when you think of the Godots? Them fighting?

SHE
No. I suppose I picture them sitting at home, on their very clean white leather sectional thingy, watching TV, and both thinking, vaguely, that they've forgotten something, but neither of them bothering to mention it and work out that they are supposed to be meeting us here for dinner!

HE
Yeah. Yeah, that is a possibility. Maybe we <u>should</u> text them.

(HE reaches for his phone, but SHE reaches to stop him.)

SHE
Maybe they've decided not to come. Maybe we're boring. Maybe we're so boring that they couldn't muster the strength to sustain them through another evening with us.

HE
No.

SHE
Are we boring?

HE
No... No.

SHE
Sometimes I wonder.

HE
No. Do you? No.

(They pause, thinking.)

SHE
We're boring when we're alone.

HE
No. I don't think so.

SHE
Well, eating dinner in the living room watching the news and Jeopardy, that's pretty boring.

HE
Everyone does that.

SHE
No, not everyone.

HE
Sure.

SHE
Seniors, maybe.

HE
Or some variation. It's called routine. Right? Everyone's boring in that sense.

SHE
I don't know.

HE
Everyone's boring in their own special way.

(SHE takes a sustained look at him.)

SHE
"Everyone's boring in their own special way" I suppose there's some comfort in that.

HE
Absolutely. And look at us tonight!

SHE
Right.

HE
We're not sitting at home eating in front of the TV.

SHE
Right!

HE
We've gone out!

SHE
We have!

HE
We're eating in public!

SHE
We are!

HE
With friends.

SHE
If they ever show up.

HE
Yeah.

(They pause. SHE looks up, above and behind him.)

SHE
Of course, they have a fricking TV here anyway.

HE
(looks around.)
Oh yeah.

SHE
With the sound turned off.

HE
That's… that's weird. I hadn't noticed.

HE continues to look toward the TV.

SHE
Why on earth would they do that?

HE
Yeah. Strange.

HE keeps looking at the TV.

SHE
Why would they subject everyone to TV since we've finally broken away from the damn thing for a change?

HE
Probably so it's not too much change. The TV is... reassuring.

(HE keeps looking at it. SHE observes him.)

SHE
Look away.

HE keeps looking.

HE
Huh?

SHE
Look away.

HE keeps looking.

HE
I'm just... It's just… it's… try to see… what… that… what...

SHE
Look the f--k away.

HE looks at her.

HE
Okay.

SHE
Pretend it's not there.

HE
Okay. Okay. Yes.
(glances quickly at the TV)
Okay.

SHE
I am really, truly, getting really fucking hungry. Maybe they have some fortune cookies by the till.

HE
No, it's an Indian restaurant. Why would they have fortune cookies?

SHE
Damn, you're right.

(HE looks up at the TV. Pause. SHE clears her throat.
HE looks back at her and turns his back to the TV.)

SHE (CONT'D)
How long do you think it'll take if I order off the menu?

HE
Who can say? They're pretty busy.

SHE
The Godots better show up soon -- that "nice" waitress is looking like she's about to drag us to that table for two by the washrooms.

HE looks.

HE
Where? Oh. You know, I'm gonna zip to the washroom, since we're waiting if you'll hold our place in line.
SHE looks behind them.

SHE
What line? There is no line.

HE
Well, not right now, no, but… if we both leave when we come back, there could be a line.

SHE
But the waitress knows we were here first.

HE
But the people in line won't know that.

SHE
We would tell them. I would tell them.

HE
Okay, if you want to go, you go first and then I'll go when you get back.

SHE
I don't want to go at all.

HE
Okay, well, then, I'm going, back in a jiff.

(SHE watches him go.)

SHE
(in monologue)
What is it with him? He peed just before we left the house. He should have his prostate checked. Do they really still do it with a finger? Up... up the...the. No. Probably very high tech now. Robot finger. Yeah... Robot finger.

(SHE glances briefly at the TV.)

SHE (CONT'D)
Okay, now people are gonna think I'm dining alone. I don't really mind. A woman of mystery. A traveler, maybe. Sometimes I'd rather be alone. I'd rather be alone than feel like this like I feel tonight. Why are we here? We should have stayed home like the Godots. And I like Jeopardy. Although it's not what it used to be. Maybe we're not what we used to be. I don't know. I feel...I feel like somehow we've stopped... moving. Stopped caring. Stopped loving. Really loving. I don't know. I don't know. We tell each other we do, even if it's more of a salutation. 'See you at six. Love you.' Might as well be saying 'Drive carefully' or 'Don't slip on the ice.' We haven't actually talked about love since the days when it was new to us. I should ask him. I should ask him tonight. 'Do. You. Still. Love. Me?' Do I dare? What would he say? And if he asks me? If he asks me, what would I say? What would I say? Here he comes. I'll just ask him, 'Do you still love me?' Right now. I'll ask him. It's now or never. Alright. Here it goes...

HE
The Godots are here!

SHE
What?

HE
They're here, just around the corner.

SHE
No.

HE
The Godots have been waiting for us.

SHE
They've been here all along? Have they ordered?

HE
They're both gonna have the buffet.

SHE
Let's make it four.

SHE signals to a waitress.

SHE (CONT'D)
Two more buffets over here. Two more buffets.

SHE and HE hurry across the stage.

HE
Hey, are you okay? You had a strange look on your face just now.

SHE
Me? No, I'm fine. I'm absolutely fine. Let's eat. Let's eat!

(SHE and HE hurry off.)

CURTAIN

CONTRIBUTORS

KAREN STARRETT

Karen Starrett has an honors B.A. from Douglass College, Rutgers University, and she continued her studies at the School of Visual Arts. In addition to being a painter, Starrett is a teaching artist for people with dementia. Her organization, Creative Aging Arts LLC, facilitates art workshops in adult care communities. Her curriculum's foundation is a continuation of her life as an artist, her love of personal imagery, and the use of paint, paper, and mixed media. She describes painting as "a body-centered action" that continues to be "an expression of [her] life." After working in collage for many years, she came to painting in 2005 in response to a life-threatening ovarian cancer diagnosis, the focus of her early paintings. Karen Starrett's paintings have been exhibited in solo and group exhibitions. She has won awards, received a grant from The Puffin Foundation, and, in 2019, curated *Art & Healing: expressions of trauma and gratitude* at The Monmouth Museum.

karenstarrett.com

ANTHONY AFAIRO NZE

Anthony Afairo Nze is a 21-year-old graphic design student from Indiana. He spends most of his free time drawing art pieces, comic strips and practicing graphic design.

instagram.com/Afairosgallery instagram.com/Recklesspeoplecomics

SARAH PASSINHAS-BERGMAN

Sarah Passinhas-Bergman cannot find her copy of *Fornes' Enter the*

Night anywhere, but she thinks you should read it when you have time. She graduated from Cal Poly San Luis Obispo in 2019. She published one short story, *Anthropologists,* (*Byzantium,* 2019), and won a playwriting contest for her one-act, *Rinse Cycle,* which premiered in the Spring 2018 One-Act Festival. Passinhas-Bergman by day is a library assistant and an intern with Arlekin Players Theatre. *Iris Literary Journal* is her first non-campus-affiliated published work. She currently lives in Massachusetts.

J V BIRCH

J V Birch lives in Adelaide, South Australia. Her poems have appeared in several anthologies, including *Balancing Act and Other Poems* (named after her poem), *Sentinel Champions, Australian Love Poems, The Emma Press Anthology of Aunts, Australian Poetry Member's Anthology,* and *The Hunter Writers Centre Grieve Anthology*. Her work has also featured in journals and magazines, including *Ink, Sweat and Tears, Coffin Bell, Australian Poetry Journal, Plumwood Mountain, The Poetry Shed, Not Very Quiet, Zoomorphic, Magma, Cordite,* and *Mslexia*. She has been a three-time winner in a poetry category of mindshare's Creative Writing Awards and a prize winner in The Molotov Cocktail Shadow Award. *Ginninderra Press* has published three of her chapbooks – *Smashed glass at midnight* in their Picaro Poets series, and *What the water & moon gave me* and *A bellyful of roses* in their Pocket Poets series – and her first full-length collection, *more than here.*

jvbirch.com

STEPHANIE BLANCH-BYER

Stephanie Blanch-Byer is a New York City Public High School Special Education Teacher with more than 15 years of experience. Born and raised on Chicago's Westside, poetry has been her way of "sorting out her stuff" since the third grade. She is the founder of the Black Gyrl Collective (BGC). Besides curating their own weekly writing space, community write-ins, and monthly BGC poetry events, Stephanie has also facilitated writing and wellness workshops as a tool for healing for the Catalyst: Ed Network's Black Woman's Journey to Reclamation Series. Her multimedia poetry and prose can be found at the exhibition, Blacktivism: The New Generation in Washington, DC (since 2016). Some of her works have also been shared at BlackOut (2020); La Mama Poetry Electric: Tribute to Toni Morrison(2019), Harlem Pride: Speak Your Myne(2019), Downbraiding: A Reading in Three Voices(2019), Still BOLD (2019) Poets on the Verge(2018), La Mama: Women Writers/Resist (2017) NYC Black Pride(2016), Womyn & Words at the Lesbian HerStory Archives (2015), Latinos NYC: Nuyorican Cafe (2015), and Women of the African Diaspora (2014).

freeeedomtour.com

GAVIN BOURKE

Gavin Bourke grew up in the suburb of Tallaght in West Dublin. He holds a B.A. in Humanities from Dublin City University, an M.A, in Modern Drama Studies, and a Higher Diploma in Information Studies from University College Dublin. His poetry appears in a number of publications, including *Crossways Literary Magazine, Qutub Minar Review International Literary Magazine,* and *A New Ulster.* In 2016, his work was shortlisted for The Redline Book Festival Poetry Award. In 2019, he read at the Siarsceál Literary Festival; his poem, *Louisburgh, County Memory,* was highly commended in the Johnathon Swift Creative Writing Awards, his poem *Ag Iarraidh, a Churam Mo Intinn Bhun Os Cionn,* was shortlisted for The Manchester Irish Language Group International Poetry Competition, and his first book of poetry, *sixty pages,* was shortlisted for the International Hedgehog Poetry Press (UK) Full Fat Collection Poetry Competition. His book *Toward Human* (Hedgehog Poetry Press, 2020) is the winner of the international Nicely Folded Paper Trois International Poetry Collection Competition. Gavin continues to write and work County Meath with his spouse, Annemarie.

S. T. BRANT

S. T. Brant is a teacher from Las Vegas. He has publications in/coming from *EcoTheo, Door is a Jar, Santa Clara Review, Rain Taxi, New South, Green Mountains Review, Another Chicago Magazine, Ekstasis, 8 Poems,* a few others.

twitter.com/terriblebinth
instagram.com/shanelemagne/

JILL BRONFMAN

Jill Bronfman is a professor, lawyer, non-profit worker, and parent. Her work has been accepted for publication in *Rougarou, Ruminate Magazine, The Write Launch, The Decadent Review, The Halcyone, 82 Review, The Passed Note, Storgy, Verbal, Kallisto Gaia, Main Street Rag, High Desert, Flying Ketchup, Carcosa, Genre: Urban Arts, Ripples in Space, Mothers Always Write, Talking Writing, Coffin Bell Journal, Flock, Wanderlust Journal, Quiet Lightning,* and law and technical books and periodicals. She has performed her work in Poets in the Parks, The Basement Series, and LitQuake, and had her story about a middle-aged robot produced as a podcast.

ANN-MARIE BROWN

Ann-Marie Brown is a Canadian painter currently working out of a studio tucked between the forest & the Pacific Ocean. Her oil and encaustic paintings have been exhibited across Canada & the United States and found their way into public, private & corporate collections.

annmariebrownpaintings.com

LIN MARSHALL BRUMMELS

Lin Marshall Brummels, a native Nebraskan and life-long resident grew up on a farm at the edge of the Nebraska Sandhills. Brummels earned a Psychology BA from the University of Nebraska-Lincoln, an MS in Rehabilitation Counseling from Syracuse University, and is a licensed mental health counselor in private practice. She was Director of Counseling at Wayne State College for 39 years, where she provided mental health counseling to students and supervised beginning counselors. She is an environmentalist who often finds mental health solutions in the garden. Her poetry has appeared in *Concho River Review, Iris Literary Journal, Oakwood, Paddlefish, Pinyon Review, Plainsongs, Poet Lore, San Pedro River Review, The Sea Letter, Nebraska Life Magazine,* and several anthologies. Her poetry chapbooks are

"Cottonwood Strong" and "Hard Times," winner of a 2016 Nebraska Book Award. Brummels' first full-length poetry collection is with Scurfpea Publishing (2021).

twitter.com/linbrummmels

ANNA CITRINO

Anna Citrino grew up in San Diego County and taught abroad in international schools in Turkey, Kuwait, Singapore, Saudi Arabia, India, and the United Kingdom. Her current home is Soquel, California, where she enjoys raising her own food and learning to draw. Anna's work has appeared in various literary journals, including *Bellowing Ark, Canary, Earth's Daughters, Evening Street Review, Paterson Literary Review, Porter Gulch Review, phren-z, La Piccioletta Barca, Rockvale Review, and Spillway,* among other publications. Nominated for a Pushcart Prize in 2019, Citrino is the author of *A Space Between,* and two chapbooks, *Saudade* and *To Find a River.*

annacitrino.com

JANE COSTAIN

Jane Costain is a freelance writer and poet. Although she has been writing poetry for many years, she has only recently begun to publish some of her poems in various journals. Her chapbook, *Small Windows,* was published by Main Street Rag in 2018.

KRISTA MARIE DEBEHNKE

Krista Marie DeBehnke is a poet and playwright originally from Milwaukee, Wisconsin but currently lives, writes, and teaches in Augusta, Georgia. Her work has appeared in or is forthcoming in *Masque & Spectacle, Saranac Review, What Are Birds? Journal, Up the Staircase Quarterly, Apeiron Review, Rock & Sling, Portland Review, Bateau Ivre,* and *Railtown Almanac,* among others. She writes and produces two horror podcasts, *Dr. Scarelove* and *Haunting Season,* with her husband, Drew Attana.

drscarelove.com

RC DEWINTER

RC deWinter's poetry is widely anthologized, notably in *Uno: A Poetry Anthology (Xlibris, 4/2002), New York City Haiku (NY Times, 2/2017), Cowboys & Cocktails (Brick Street, 4/2019), Nature In The Now (Tiny Seed Press, 8/2019), Coffin Bell Two (March 2020), Other Worldly Women Press 2020 Summer Anthology: a Headrest for Your Soul (June 2020)*, in print in *2River, Adelaide, Door Is A Jar, Event, Genre Urban Arts, Gravitas, Kansas City Voices, Meat For Tea: The Valley Review, The Minnesota Review, Night Picnic Journal, Prairie Schooner, Reality Break Press, Southword* among others and appears in numerous online literary journals.

rc-dewinter.pixels.com/

DONNARKEVIC

donnarkevic lives in Buckhannon, WV, and has an MFA from National University. Recent poetry has appeared in *Triggerfish, Nassau Review,* and *About Place Journal.* donnarkevic is a Best of the Net and Pushcart Prize nominee whose plays have received readings in Chicago, New York, Virginia, and West Virginia. Poetry Collections include *Laundry*, (Main Street Rag, 2005). *Admissions,* a book of poems (FutureCycle Press, 2013), *Many Sparrows* (The Poetry Box, 2018).

KEN FARRELL

Ken Farrell's work is forthcoming or published in anthologies and journals such as *Ripples in Space, Pilgrimage, Sport Literate, Watershed Review, Coffin Bell Journal, The Piltdown Review,* and elsewhere. He holds an MFA from Texas State University and an MA from Salisbury University, and he has earned as an adjunct, cage fighter, pizzaiolo, and warehouseman. Ken is currently revising and shopping his work and responding to his daughter's challenge, who participated in NaNoWriMo. He recently began his first novel, a tale about a world where ghosts serve on juries, the sky is off-limits, and shards of souls are commodities.

WILLIAM IVOR FOWKES

William Ivor Fowkes is a playwright and author based in New York and a member of the Dramatists Guild. His plays have been presented in 24 states and the District of Columbia. Many have been published (*Dramatists Play Service, The Best 10-Minute Plays—Smith & Kraus, The Best Women's Stage Monologues and Scenes—Smith & Kraus, Clockhouse Review, The Distillery, The Paragon Journal, Statement Magazine, The Eddy, Fleas on the Dog*, and elsewhere). His fiction has been published in many journals (*Eureka Literary Magazine, The Dirty Goat, The Nassau Review, The Chariton Review, Lullwater Review, Wisconsin Review, RiverSedge, Limestone, Argestes, Soundings East, Buffalo Carp: Quad Cities Arts' Journal*, and elsewhere). He is also the author of *A Hegelian Account of Contemporary Art* (Ann Arbor: UMI Research Press). A graduate of Yale University (B.A., magna cum laude) and Northwestern University (M.A., Ph.D.), he was formerly a philosophy professor (Hobart & William Smith Colleges and Northwestern University) and a media & television executive (Showtime, HBO, CBS Records, and Time Magazine). He currently runs a playwrights' group at the Dramatists Guild in New York. He is married to music conductor Stephen Michael Smith.

williamivorfowkes.com

RAMONA GABAR

"Miracle" is part of Ramona Gabar's first volume of short stories, called "Stations." The volume is built around stories of migration, of forced relocation, of cut and run. In "Stations," destinies remain suspended for a brief moment while we witness (and weigh in on) their options. Ramona writes in Romanian, English, and French. She is currently working with her 10-year old daughter on a children's book in French.

twitter.com/RamonaGabar

instagram.com/bufnita

OLGA GONZALEZ LATAPI

Olga Gonzalez Latapi (she/her/hers) is a queer poet with an MFA in Writing from California College of the Arts. Although her writing journey started in journalism, she is now pursuing her true passion: exploring the world of poetry with a mighty pen in hand. She got her BS in Journalism at Northwestern University. Her work has been published in *Teen Voices Magazine, Sonder Midwest literary arts magazine, BARNHOUSE Literary Journal, Wild Roof Journal, Impossible Task, Genre: Urban Arts, Biscuitroot Drive, iaam.com,* and *The Nasiona Magazine,* among others. Originally from Mexico City, she currently lives in Toronto.

letolgatellyouastory.tumblr.com/
twitter.com/Olga_G_L
facebook.com/OlgaGl92

CLEO GRIFFITH

Cleo Griffith was Chair of the Editorial Board of *Song of the San Joaquin* for its first twelve years and currently sits on the Board in its 17th year. A member of the Modesto branch of the National League of American Pen Women and widely published, she lives in Salida, CA, with her cats, Amber and Neil.

JACK HALLIDAY

Jack Halliday is an author, award-winning screenwriter and producer whose work has appeared in numerous digital and print publications. Wildside Press published his first fiction collection, Kawanga/Swan and Other Mystery Stories, as their 12th "Mystery Double." His noir mystery novel, *The Big Bluff,* debuted from Solstice Publishing in 2018. His new detective fiction collection, *Finding Phyllis and Other Howard Millar Capers,* are currently available from Bold Venture Press. He lives with his wife and son in the Midwest.

jackhalliday.com

PATRICK CABELLO HANSEL

Patrick Cabello Hansel is the author of the poetry collections The Devouring Land (Main Street Rag Publishing) and Quitting Time (Atmosphere Press). He has published poems and prose in over 65 journals, including *Crannog, Ilanot Review, Hawai'i Pacific Review, Ash & Bones, RiverSedge,* and *Lunch Ticket,* and won awards from The Loft Literary Center and MN State Arts Board. His novella *Searching* was serialized in 33 issues of The Alley News. He is the editor of *The*

Phoenix of Phillips, a literary journal by and for Minneapolis's most diverse community.

spiritwound.blogspot.com/

TRACY HARRIS

Tracy Harris writes, volunteers, and studies French in St. Paul, Minnesota. Her essays have appeared in *Wraparound South, Midwestern Gothic, Lunch Ticket, the Tahoma Literary Review,* and *Mason's Road,* among others. She is a former board member of *Water-Stone Review* and participant in Cracked Walnut, a series of literary readings in the Twin Cities.

PATRICIA JOYNES

Patricia Joynes frequents the Blue Ridge Parkway, shooting nature photography. Her photos are on book covers, in annual *Blue Ridge Parkway* calendars, a National Geographic online story, and in literary journals including *County Lines* (2015-2019), *Evening Paper* (cover) *Oracle Fine Arts Review, Sunlight Press, DASH, RiverSedge, San Pedro River Review, THE SUN, Blue Mesa Review, Proud to Be: Writing by American Warriors, Camas,* and *The Closed Eye Open.*

patriciajoynes.wordpress.com/about/

JEANNE JULIAN

The Poetry Box published Jeanne Julian's full-length collection, *Like the O in Hope* (2019). Her prior publications include two chapbooks, *Blossom* and *Loss* (Longleaf Press) and *Relic and Myth* (Prolific Press). She grew up in Ohio, graduated from Allegheny College, and earned an MFA in fiction from the University of Massachusetts, Amherst. After retiring from a higher education administration career in Massachusetts, Jeanne moved with her husband to New Bern, North Carolina. There, she helped coordinate Nexus Poets' monthly open mic and Carteret Writers' speaker series. Now living in Maine, Jeanne joined the Maine Writers & Publishers Alliance. She is a co-winner of Reed Magazine's Edwin Markham Prize for Poetry (2019-20); her poems also have won awards from *The Comstock Review, Naugatuck River Review,* and the North Carolina Poetry Society. You can find her work in *Prairie Wolf Press Review, Poetry Quarterly, High Desert Journal, Lascaux Prize 2016 Anthology, pacificREVIEW, The RavensPerch, Snapdragon*, and other journals. She also regularly writes poetry book reviews for *The Main Street Rag*.

jeannejulian.com/

HARI BHAJAN KHALSA

Hari Bhajan Khalsa grew up in a small town in Central Oregon, has lived with her husband in Los Angeles for the past forty years, and is looking to return to her rural roots in the near future. Her poems have recently been published or forthcoming in *Sand Hills Literary Journal, Birdcoat Quarterly, Potomac Review, Schuylkill Valley Journal*, and *Transcend*, among others, in *The Halcyone, The Blue Earth, Gasher*, and *Zone 3*. She is the author of a chapbook, *Life in Two Parts* (*Main Street Rag*, 2010) and a book of poems, *Talk of Snow* (*Walrus*, 2015).

KIM KOLARICH

Kim Kolarich is an actress, playwright, and fiction writer from Chicago. A graduate from Columbia College, she received her acting training from the Steven Ivcich Professional Studio and studied playwriting at the Chicago Dramatists. Among her theater, television, and film credits are the Henry Jaglom films: *Festival in Cannes, Going Shopping, Hollywood Dreams*, and *Ovation*. Her plays have been produced at Circle Theatre's New Works Festival III, the Et Cetera Festival, the Experimental Theatre, The Dandelion Theatre in Chicago, and the Estrogenius Festival New York. Her play *Far Rockaway* received honorable mention and a staged reading at the Pittsburgh New Works Festival. Her full-length play, *Three Chords*, was a semifinalist for the O'Neill Playwrights Conference and Screencraft's Stageplay contest. Kim is a Pushcart Prize nominee, and her stories have appeared in *The Bridport Prize Anthology, FreeFall, Julien's Journal, 3711 Atlantic, 34th Parallel, Karamu, Rollick Magazine, After Hours, The Gap Tooth Madness, Streetwrite, Intrinsick Magazine, Paragraph Planet, The Furious Gazelle, Two Hawks Quarterly, Third Coast Magazine, Crossways Magazine*, and *Burningword Literary Journal*. She is also the recipient of the John Wood Community College Literary Award. She placed second in the

University of Chicago's Writer's Studio Fiction Contest. Her short stories have received honorable mentions for the Women in the Arts Fiction Contest, the Page Edwards Short Fiction Contest, and the CNW/Florida State Writing Competition. She was a fiction finalist for the Arts & Letters Journal of Contemporary Culture Prize and a semifinalist for the Dana Awards and the H.E. Francis Literary Competition.

PAUL KURZEJA

Paul Kurzeja is obtaining his M.A. in Creative Writing at UNC Charlotte. His is a winner of the UNCC James McGavran Award and the Elizabeth Simpson Smith Short Story Award. He was also a finalist for the Doris Betts Fiction Prize. Paul has most recently been published in *Atlantis Magazine, Boston Accent Literary Magazine* and *Terrain*. Paul and his writing have also been featured on Charlotte Readers Podcast.

RICHARD LEIST

Richard Leist has a B.A. from Franklin and Marshall College and an M.A. in Magazine Writing from S.I. Newhouse School, Syracuse University. He is a news reporter for Booth Newspapers and an editor for the U.S. Navy Atlantic Fleet monthly tabloid as well as the Editor/Publisher of the monthly tabloid for Great Lakes sailors. Richard's work has an honorable mention in Writers Digest Short Story Contest, and he is currently completing two full-length thrillers.

KY LI

ky li has a MA in poetry and creative writing and is an avid hiker, cyclist & yogi in Louisville, Kentucky. His whose work has appeared in *Brittle Star, Dime Show Review, High Shelf Press, Nine Muses Poetry, The Bangalore Review, The Ibis Head Review, The Oddville Press, West Trade Review, Word Fountain, Timberline Review, Sheepshead Review,* and the books *Six Voices and Six Voices Two,* published in 2017 and 2019 by BlackThorn Press.

SM LINDBERG

SM Lindberg lives in Denver, Colorado, with her husband and furry critters. After earning her MFA in creative nonfiction writing from Antioch University Los Angeles, she now teaches writing at two local community colleges.

twitter.com/Smlindbe

LAURA LUCAS

Laura Lucas is a Canadian poet and singer-songwriter. Laura is passionate about music, yoga, and traveling with a purpose. Her work has been published or is forthcoming in *Press 53, Burnt Pine Magazine, Snapdragon: A Journal of Art and Healing, From Whispers to Roars,* and elsewhere.

lauralucasmusic.com

BELLABIANCA LYNN

BellaBianca Lynn is a yogini-belly dancer from Massachusetts. Lynn's work has appeared/ is forthcoming in *Adelaide Magazine, Belly Dance New England Magazine, East by Northeast, Eunoia Review,* and *Soul-Lit.*

bellabiancalynn.com

AUSTIN MANCHESTER

Austin Manchester is an aspiring author and experienced bookseller living in New York City. His work has been featured by *The Literary Yard, Finding the Birds, From Whispers to Roars,* and *Please See Me.*

DON MCLELLAN

Vancouver, B.C. writer Don McLellan has worked as a journalist in Canada, South Korea, and Hong Kong. He's had two story collections published, *In the Quiet After Slaughter* (Libros Libertad, 2008, a ReLit Award finalist), and *Brunch with the Jackals* (Thistledown Press, 2015). He's been short and longlisted for the Commonwealth Short Story Prize and is a 2020 Pushcart Prize nominee. His third story collection, *Ouch: 20 stories,* is forthcoming.

donmclellan.com

LINDA MILLER

Linda Miller has worked in newspapers, magazines, and educational public relations. For the last four years, she has devoted her writing life to memoir. Her work has appeared in *The Furious Gazelle, Dead Housekeeping, Under the Gum Tree, and Coffee & Crumbs,* a blog devoted to motherhood.

CAROL LOUISE MUNN

Carol Louise Munn is a Texan who lives and writes in Houston. She earned her MFA at the University of Michigan, where she won an American Poet's prize plus a full fellowship. Her poems are published in various literary journals and anthologies, including *Poetry* and *Untameable City*. She teaches creative writing in several universities and most recently at The Woman's Institute of Houston.

MARTHA NANCE

Martha Nance is a physician in Minnesota whose iPhone is happiest when she is not at work. Work is hard. Looking around when she is outside is a pleasure. Her nature photographs have previously been published in *The Tiny Seed Journal, The Esthetic Apostle,* and *Wanderlust,* among other journals.

ROBERT NISBET

Robert Nisbet is a Welsh poet who has been published widely in Britain and the USA. In Britain, he was the winner of the 2017 Prole Pamphlet Competition with *Robeson, Fitzgerald, and Other Heroes*. In the USA, Robert is a 2020 Pushcart Prize nominee for *Cultivation*. He is also a creative writing tutor at Trinity College, Carmarthen.

LEAH OATES

Leah Oates has a B.F.A. from the Rhode Island School of Design and an M.F.A. from The School of the Art Institute of Chicago and is a Fulbright Fellow for graduate study at Edinburgh College of Art in Scotland. Oates has been in group shows in Toronto at The Gladstone

Hotel, Gallery 1313, Propeller Gallery, Papermill Gallery, Arta Gallery, Neilson Park Creative Centre, Gerrard Art Space, Connections Gallery, and Wychwood Barns Community Gallery. Oates has had press in *Art Toronto, Junto Magazine, Magazine 43, Underexposed Magazine, Ruminate Journal, Mud Season Review, dArt Magazine, The Tulane Review, The Six Hundred JournalBlue Mesa Review, Friends of the Artist, GASHER Journal, Flumes Literary Journal, and the 805 Lit + Art Journal.* Oates has had solo shows at Black Cat Artspace, Susan Eley Fine Art, The MTA Lightbox Project at 42nd Street, The Arsenal Gallery in Central Park, The Center for Book Arts, Henry Street Settlement and A Taste of Art Gallery and Tomasulo Gallery in New Jersey, Real Art Ways in Connecticut, Sara Nightingale Gallery in Water Mill, Long Island and the Sol Mednick Gallery at the Philadelphia University of the Arts. Oates has had solo shows nationally at Anchor Graphics, Artemisia Gallery, and Woman Made Gallery in Chicago and internationally at Galerie Joella in Turku, Finland.

leahoates.com

ERNST PERDRIEL

Ernst Perdriel was born in Quebec, Canada. He lives in the Eastern Townships region, Quebec, Canada. As a multi-field artist, designer, and horticulturist, he has participated in solo and group exhibitions in visual arts since 1995. He has contributed to numerous publications since 1992 as a writer, illustrator, artist, and photographer.

ernstperdriel.com

SAMANTHA PILECKI

Samantha Pilecki is the winner of the Haunted Waters Press Short Shorts Competition, the Writing District's monthly contest, and was a finalist in both the Writer's Digest Short Story contest and New Millennium Writings contest. Her work has appeared in *Kansas City Voices, New Lit Salon Press, Timberline Review,* and *Yemassee*. She works as a librarian.

spilecki1044.wixsite.com/home

SHANA ROSS

Shana Ross is a poet and playwright with a BA and MBA from Yale University. She bought her first computer working the graveyard shift in a wind chime factory and now pays her bills as a consultant and leadership expert. Since resuming her writing career in 2018, she has accumulated over 40 publication credits, including *Anapest Journal, Chautauqua Journal, Ghost City Review, Mad Scientist Journal, The Sunlight Press,* and *Writers Resist*. She is the recipient of a 2019 Parent-Writer Fellowship to Martha's Vineyard Institute of Creative Writing and serves as an editor for *Luna Station Quarterly*.

MARY KAY RUMMEL

Mary Kay Rummel was poet laureate of Ventura County, CA, from 2014-2017. Blue Light Press of San Francisco published *Cypher Garden* and her ninth book of poetry, *Nocturnes: Between Flesh and Stone*. *The Lifeline Trembles* won the 2014 Blue Light Poetry Prize. Her other books include *The Illuminations* (Cherry Grove Editions), *This Body She's Entered* (New Rivers Press, Minnesota Voices award), *Love in the End* (Bright Hill Press Chapbook Award), *Green Journey, Red Bird* (Loonfeather press), and *The Long Journey into North* published (Juniper Press). She co-edited *Psalms of Cinder & Silt*, community poems by survivors of recent California fires published by Solo Press. She divides her time between Minneapolis, MN, and Ventura, CA.

marykayrummel.com

JOEL SAVISHINSKY

Joel Savishinsky is an anthropologist and gerontologist. His books include *The Trail of the Hare: Environment and Stress in a Sub-Arctic Community, The Ends of Time: Life and Work in A Nursing Home,* and *Breaking the Watch: The Meanings of Retirement in America*. The latter two both won the Gerontological Society of America's Kalish Award for Innovative Publishing. His poetry and nonfiction have appeared, or are forthcoming, in *Anthropology and Humanism Quarterly, The Avocet, Awake in The World, The Berkshire Review, Blood and Thunder, Cirque, Crosscurrents, Down in the Dirt, Evening Street Review, From Whispers to Roars, Muddy River Poetry Review, The New York Times, Page-Boy, Passager, The Pharos, Raw Art Review, The Third Eye, Windfall, and*

Xanadu. He lives in Seattle, helping to raise five grandchildren and as much political trouble as he can. He considers himself a recovering academic and an unrepentant activist for social justice.

ROBIN SCHLAHT

Robin Schlaht is a writer and filmmaker based in Regina, Canada. Born and raised in a small prairie town, Robin has traveled the world to make and present his films, including at such prestigious festivals as Toronto International Film Festival and South-by-Southwest. His works include documentary and fiction films and interactive new media, and scripts for live theatre.

facebook.com/robin.schlaht

D. N. SIMMERS

d. n. simmers is an online editor of Fine Lines. His first of his three published books was a finalist in the Fred Cogswell Award. His U.S. publications include *California Quarterly, The Common Ground Review, Poets Touchstone,* and his international publications include *Tears in the Fence* (UK) *Salzburg Poetry Review,* and *Van Gogh's Ear* (France). His fourth book comes out in 2021.

WILLIAM R. STODDART

William R. Stoddart is a poet and story writer who lives in the suburbs of Pittsburgh, Pennsylvania. His work has appeared in *Maryland Literary Review, Adirondack Review, Ruminate Magazine, Pedestal Magazine, Neologism Poetry Journal,* and *Nine Muses Poetry*.

TIM SUERMONDT

Tim Suermondt's sixth full-length book of poems, *A Doughnut and The Great Beauty Of The World,* is with MadHat Press (2021). His work also appears in *Poetry, Ploughshares, Prairie Schooner, The Georgia Review, Bellevue Literary Review, Stand Magazine, December magazine, On the Seawall, Poet Lore,* and *Plume,* among many others. He lives in Cambridge, MA, with his wife, the poet Pui Ying Wong.

facebook.com/tim.suermondt

ELIZABETH TEMPLEMAN

Elizabeth Templeman lives, writes, and works in the Central Interior of British Columbia. A collection of her essays, *Notes from the Interior,* was published in 2003 by Oolichan Books; individual essays and book reviews have appeared in *The Globe & Mail* ("Facts & Arguments"). She also has work in anthologies and in journals, which include *Room Magazine* and *Eastern Iowa Review.*

DENISE THOMPSON-SLAUGHTER

Denise Thompson-Slaughter was born in Washington, D.C., worked her way through college at the University of Maryland and Rutgers University, where she received a B.A. in English. She spent several decades after that as an academic editor, mother, and writer. She lives with her history-professor husband in western New York. Her published work includes two books of poetry, *Elemental* (Plain-View Press, 2010), and *Sixty-ish: Full Circle* (Spirited Muse Press, 2017), a mystery novella set in Nova Scotia, *Mystery Gifts* (Spirited Muse Press, 2018), two short stories, and a handful of brief memoir pieces. Her other publications include poems in *Nine Cloud Journal* and *Tipton Poetry Journal.*

facebook.com/DenneeDesk

MORRIE WARSHAWSKI

Morrie Warshawski grew up in Kansas City, received BA/MA in English from Univ. of So. Calif., and attended the Graduate Writers Workshop in Poetry at the Univ. of Iowa. Morrie Recently retired from freelance consulting with nonprofits and independent filmmakers and is currently writing, drawing, painting, collaging, and growing tomatoes.

ALAN WELTZIEN

Alan Weltzien, a newly retired English professor from Montana, has published lots of articles, two chapbooks, and ten books. These include three poetry collections, the most recent, *Rembrandt in the Stairwell* (2016). His biography of Montana novelist Thomas Savage, *Savage West: The Life and Fiction of Thomas Savage,* is with the University of Nevada Press (2020). Weltzien has had several poems published in sundry journals and is working on a fourth collection. He still loves to ski in winter and hike in summer, and travel internationally with his wife.

SHARON WHITEHILL

Sharon Whitehill is a retired English professor from Michigan who now lives in Florida. Publications include two biographies, two memoirs, two poetry chapbooks (Cosmographia Books, 2018 and Finishing Line Press, 2019), and *A Dream of Wide Water*, a full collection of poems from Atmosphere Press (2020).

CYNTHIA YATCHMAN

Cynthia Yatchman is a Seattle based painter/printmaker and art instructor teaching art to adults, children, and families. Her work is housed in numerous public and private collections and has been shown in California, Connecticut, New York, Indiana, Michigan, Oregon, and Wyoming. She exhibits extensively in the Northwest.

facebook.com/cynthia.yatchman

www.ingramcontent.com/pod-product-compliance
Lightning Source LLC
Chambersburg PA
CBHW061118100726
47911CB00013B/591

* 9 7 8 1 7 3 5 6 9 2 3 2 6 *